A Brav

GLOBAL ISSUES IN

This new series of short, accessible think-pieces deals with the ing global issues of relevance to humanity today. Intended for the enquiring reader and social activists in the North and the South, as well as students, the books explain what is at stake and question conventional ideas and policies. Drawn from many different parts of the world, the series' authors pay particular attention to the needs and interests of ordinary people, whether living in the rich industrial or the developing countries. They all share a common objective – to help stimulate new thinking and social action in the opening years of the new century.

Global Issues in a Changing World is a joint initiative by Zed Books in collaboration with a number of partner publishers and non-governmental organizations around the world. By working together, we intend to maximize the relevance and availability of the books published in the series.

Participating NGOs

Both ENDS, Amsterdam
Catholic Institute for International Relations, London
Corner House, Sturminster Newton
Council on International and Public Affairs, New York
Dag Hammarskjöld Foundation, Uppsala
Development GAP, Washington DC
Focus on the Global South, Bangkok
Inter Pares, Ottawa
Public Interest Research Centre, Delhi
Third World Network, Penang
Third World Network–Africa, Accra
World Development Movement, London

About this Series

'Communities in the South are facing great difficulties in coping with global trends. I hope this brave new series will throw much needed light on the issues ahead and help us choose the right options.'

MARTIN KHOR, *Director,*
Third World Network, Penang

'There is no more important campaign than our struggle to bring the global economy under democratic control. But the issues are fearsomely complex. This Global Issues series is a valuable resource for the committed campaigner and the educated citizen.'

BARRY COATES, *Director,*
World Development Movement (WDM)

'Zed Books has long provided an inspiring list about the issues that touch and change people's lives. The Global Issues series is another dimension of Zed's fine record, allowing access to a range of subjects and authors that, to my knowledge, very few publishers have tried. I strongly recommend these new, powerful titles and this exciting series.'

JOHN PILGER, *author*

'We are all part of a generation that actually has the means to eliminate extreme poverty world-wide. Our task is to harness the forces of globalization for the benefit of working people, their families and their communities – that is our collective duty. The Global Issues series makes a powerful contribution to the global campaign for justice, sustainable and equitable development, and peaceful progress.'

GLENYS KINNOCK, MEP

About the Author

VANDANA SHIVA is a world-renowned environmental leader and activist. Director of the Research Foundation for Science, Technology and Ecology, an independent institute dedicated to research on significant ecological and social issues in close partnership with local communities, she is also a leader in the International Forum on Globalization along with Ralph Nader and Jeremy Rifkin. In 1991, she founded Navdanya, a national movement to protect the diversity and integrity of living resources, especially native seeds. One of the most provocative and dynamic thinkers on the environment, she won the Right Livelihood Award, also known as the alternative Nobel Peace Prize, in 1993. Dr Shiva is the author of many books, including *Biopiracy: The Plunder of Nature and Knowledge, Monocultures of the Mind, The Violence of the Green Revolution* and *Staying Alive*. She is also Associate Editor of *The Ecologist*.

A GLOBAL ISSUES TITLE

PROTECT OR PLUNDER?

Understanding Intellectual Property Rights

VANDANA SHIVA

ZED BOOKS
London & New York

UNIVERSITY PRESS LTD
Dhaka

WHITE LOTUS CO. LTD
Bangkok

FERNWOOD PUBLISHING LTD
Halifax, Nova Scotia

DAVID PHILIP
Cape Town

This book was first published in India with the title
Patents: Myths & Reality by Penguin Books India (P) Ltd.,
11 Community Centre, Panchsheel Park, New Delhi 110 017, India,
in 2001

Protect or Plunder was first published in 2001 by

In Bangladesh: The University Press Ltd, Red Crescent Building,
114, Motijheel C/A, PO Box 2611, Dhaka 1000

In Burma, Cambodia, Laos, Thailand and Vietnam:
White Lotus Co. Ltd, GPO Box 1141, Bangkok 10501, Thailand

In Canada: Fernwood Publishing Ltd, PO Box 9409, Station A,
Halifax, Nova Scotia, Canada B3K 5S3

In Southern Africa: David Philip Publishers (Pty Ltd),
208 Werdmuller Centre, Claremont 7735, South Africa

In the rest of the world:
Zed Books Ltd, 7 Cynthia Street, London N1 9JF, UK and
Room 400, 175 Fifth Avenue, New York, NY 10010, USA

Distributed in the USA exclusively by Palgrave, a division of
St Martin's Press, LLC, 175 Fifth Avenue, New York, NY 10010

Copyright © Vandana Shiva 2001

Cover designed by Andrew Corbett
Typeset in AGaramond by Eleven Arts, Delhi-35
Printed and bound in the United Kingdom by Cox & Wyman, Reading

A catalogue record for this book is available from the British Library
US CIP data is available from the Library of Congress
Canadian CIP data is available from the National Library of Canada

ISBN 1 55266 066 4 Pb (Canada)
ISBN 0 86486 514 7 Pb (Southern Africa)
ISBN 1 84277 108 6 Hb (Zed Books)
ISBN 1 84277 109 4 Pb (Zed Books)

Contents

Introduction:

Patents—An Ethical Crisis

UNTIL THE 1980s, PATENTS did not intrude into our everyday lives. The only people concerned about patents were therefore inventors as patent applicants, patent examiners and patent lawyers. Two events in the 1980s have changed this forever and have transformed the 'patent' into a critical issue that impinges upon the life of the common man. The first was a US Supreme Court decision to treat life as an invention and hence allow the US Patent Office to grant patents on life. The second was the introduction of patents and intellectual property rights (IPRs) in the Uruguay Round of GATT by the US.

Consider the following:

The first mammalian patent was granted on 12 April 1988 by the US Patents Office to DuPont for a mouse where infected chicken and human genes had been engineered into the mouse's permanent gene line to give it cancer. The 'onco mouse' patent held by DuPont was supposed to have helped find cancer cures, but it did not. Though the onco mouse is referred to as the 'Harvard Mouse' because research was done on it in Harvard, it can more appropriately be called the 'DuPont Mouse' because DuPont holds the patent. The patent licensed to DuPont is extraordinarily broad, wherein DuPont has patent ownership of any animal species—be it mice, rats, cats, or chimpanzees—whose gene lines are engineered to contain a variety of cancer-causing genes. The patent may well be among the broadest ever granted. DuPont thus markets the world's first patented animal, duly trademarked as the Onco Mouse.

A sheep named Tracy, is a 'biotechnological invention' of the scientists of Pharmaceutical Proteins Ltd. (PPL). Tracy is called a 'mammalian cell bioreactor' because, through the introduction of human genes, her mammary glands have been engineered to produce a protein for the pharmaceutical industry. And Ron James, then Director of PPL, is on record for stating that 'the mammary gland is a very good factory'. But to replicate Tracy, animal cloning was necessary. The scientists of PPL and Roslin Institute therefore 'created' Dolly, who was of course patented as an 'invention' of Roslin and the property of PPL.

A US firm Biocyte has a patent on all umblical cord cells from foetuses and newborn babies.

Another US company, Myriad Pharmaceuticals, has patented the breast cancer gene and has a monopoly on all diagnostic use of this patented gene.

Researchers at the National Institute of Health (NIH) in the UK patented a method for gene therapy, which was licensed to Genetic Therapy, who in turn sold it for $ 395 million to Sandoz, which later merged with Ciba Geigy to form Novartis. Thus one of the world's 'gene' giants has exclusive 'property' rights to a therapy evolved in the public domain.

In 1994, Amgen bought the patent for the so-called

obesity gene from Rockefeller University for $ 90 million. Given that Americans spend $ 30 billion annually on diet pills and weight loss programmes, the patent on the obesity gene can spin billions in a society where the industrial food system itself is geared to causing obesity.

In 1995, the US government gave itself a patent for a cell line drawn from the Hagahai people of Papua New Guinea.

Genset, a French company, has an agreement with the Chinese government to collect and patent DNA from tribes in remote regions.

Thus, today, companies, commercial laboratories, universities, researchers and more particularly governments—all seem to be in a 'high-stakes scavenger hunt' to collect 'patents' which can be sold for billions of dollars. As a result, the end of the twentieth century saw patents being granted for indigenous knowledge and plants and also for microorganisms, genes, animals, and even human cells and proteins.

The Trade Related Intellectual Property Rights (TRIPs) Agreement of GATT/WTO has globalized US-style patent laws. This has far-reaching consequences and impacts not only on our capacity to provide for our basic needs of food and medicine, but also on democracy and sovereignty. The universalization of patents to cover all subject matter, including life forms, has resulted in patents invading our forests and farms, our kitchens, and our medicinal plant gardens. Patents are now granted not just for machines but for life forms and biodiversity; not just for new inventions but for the knowledge of our grandmothers. Indigenous knowledge which India has used over centuries for everyday needs—*neem, haldi, karela, jamun, kali mirch, bhu-amla* and hundreds of other plants used in food and medicine—are in imminent danger of being patented by the western world for commercial gain. This is tantamount to biopiracy. And contrary to popular perception, western-style IPR systems, especially US patent laws, far from preventing intellectual piracy; seem to in fact promote it, even at times violating human rights.

The western patents lobby would however have us believe that patents are necessary for growth and high standards of living in free markets which are realized through technology generation. IPRs help stimulate investment, particularly foreign direct investment (FDI), technology transfer from North to South, and research and innovation, by allowing inventors to recoup R&D costs. Essentially then the public benefits of patenting and disclosure far outweigh the costs of artificial monopolies in the marketplace.

The real picture however couldn't be more different. IPRs have been used for plain 'political coercion' by industrial countries, particularly the US. By the late 1970s and 1980s the US government had acknowledged that a structural technology gap was seriously emerging between its economy and Japan's. Therefore, policy was directed to aggressively freeze the artificial advantage still enjoyed by American industry through an expansive foreign IPR policy. A survey carried out in the US in 1984 bears this out. Over eighty per cent of the companies contacted indicated that 'blocking technical areas' with no intention of working the invention was a prime motive for patenting. Patents are described as 'trump cards' to negotiate licences. In other words, the patent system 'regulates' competition. It does not necessarily stimulate technology generation, much less diffusion.

Now let us take a look at the second part of the argument viz. that these IPR systems are essential for fuelling national economic growth and investment. The R&D spending by biotechnology corporations belies this. They have been spending over $ 7 billion per year on R&D, and in 1995 alone over $ 12 billion was invested in the sector, despite weak or uncertain patent protection in many of the world's largest markets, including the EU. The profit motive without IPR props thus appears to be working well enough even in the high-tech, high-risk R&D sector. This illustrates then that there is no correlation between investment and IPR, just as there is no confirmed correlation between investment in R&D and economic growth.

Further, foreign direct investment is concentrated in the hands of a small number of companies and flows within the same company across borders. Ten developing countries alone absorb eight per cent of all FDI flowing to the South. This must be weighted against payment of royalties by all developing countries to foreign IPR-holders which drains precious reserves. Not surprisingly, an estimated seventy per cent of the global payment of royalties and licence fees comprises transactions between parent MNCs and their foreign affiliates.

The contention that patenting innovations allows inventors to recoup R&D costs is also a shaky one. Empirical evidence shows that in developed countries industry recoups fifteen to twenty per cent of its R&D costs through patents whereas in a country like India, the figure for a domestic inventor is 0.5 to two per cent.

IPRs are essentially a market distortion, a government sanctioned monopoly and subsidy. IPRs put territorial borders around technologies and other inventions so that firms can capture higher profits. In the long term, a strong IPR system can result in price discriminations and many market-distorting practices like patent pooling, tied-up sales, cross licensing and refusal to licence.

Patents are then intrinsically conflict laden. They embody conflicts between individual rights and the public interest. Patent systems are sites of a basic conflict between private ownership, creation of monopolies and private benefits against public interest and the social benefits of science and technology. Due to the inherent conflict between private and public interest, patent laws that are strong for protecting the private interest are thus weak for protecting the public interest. However, there is no 'strong' or 'weak' patent law in an absolute sense. Strength and weakness are basically relative to the interest being protected. The one-sided reference to 'strong systems' in the debate on IPRs in GATT has an underlying, tacit assumption that only corporate rights count.

Patents for living organisms impoverish human society ethically, ecologically and economically, though they bring commercial gains to a handful of corporations. If human society, in all its diversity, has to be ethically, ecologically and economically enriched, alternatives to patents have to be evolved. Patents reflect human arrogance, treating scientists as 'creators' of living organisms. Reward for innovation in these areas needs to be based on the recognition of the creativity and generative structures intrinsic to all living organisms.

Patents give the patent holder the exclusive right to his invention covering the making, rising, exercising, selling or distribution of the patented article or substance, as well as using and exercising the patented method or process of manufacturing an article or substance. In the case of patents on life, this implies that a patent holder can prevent others from making or using patented seeds, plants and animals. Since living resources and life forms 'make' themselves, and farmers have always saved their seeds and retained their calves, seed saving and exchange is treated as 'intellectual property theft' in western-style patent laws.

Patents also reflect the arrogance of western civilization, as in the case of patents on *neem*. The properties of *neem* that make it useful as a biopesticide have been known and utilized in India for centuries. They were not an invention of the scientists, who have been granted patents for *neem* biopesticide. Such intellectual property rights are in fact intellectual piracy rights. To avoid such piracy, it is essential that the collective innovation of Third World communities be recognized.

While colonial laws safeguarded markets in the colonies for foreign traders and foreign investors, sovereign laws in the Third World, like the 1970 Patent Act of India, have had to stake an equitable balance between the interests of the investor and those of consumers, and to ensure that monopolistic and restrictive practices do not hinder scientific and technological development and interrupt the growth of industry. The sovereign laws of Third World countries have been drafted to address the reality that industrialized countries have used patent systems for preventing indigenous industrial production in the Third World and maintaining it purely as a market for industrialized country products. But the changes being forced on India by TRIPs undermine these public interest safeguards and create new conflicts. With these changes, the fundamental rights and basic needs of the Indian people will be undermined in three ways. Firstly, patent monopolies will lead to increase in prices of commodities like medicines. Secondly, patenting of indigenous knowledge will make seeds and medicines inaccessible to the poor whose survival will be threatened. (See chapter on Biopiracy.) Thirdly, patenting of life forms and biodiversity will erode the sovereign power of the Third World to their resources and will generate ethical problems related to patenting of life. (See chapter on Threats to Biodiversity.) The pressure to have a globally enforceable uniform patent system is not justified on the basis of empirical evidence of the impact of patents on the public good, especially in the Third World.

The ethical issues inherent in the patenting of life have been questioned by many. Senator Mark Hatfield, a leader in the US Congressional fight against animal patenting, summed up the argument thus: 'The patenting of animals brings up the central ethical issue of reverence for life. Will future generations follow the ethic of this patent policy and view life as mere chemical manufacture and invention with no grater value or meaning than industrial products? Or will a reverence for life ethic prevail over the temptation to turn God-created life into reduced objects of commerce?'

But as we can see, patenting is not confined merely to animals. Take for example John Moore, who had been undergoing treatment for cancer of the spleen at the University of California hospital. In 1984 his doctor patented his cell line without his consent. The 'Mo cell line' was then sold to pharmaceutical giant Sandoz. Estimates of the cell line's ultimate worth have exceeded $3 billion. When Moore challenged his doctor's appropriation of his cell line, the California Court of Appeals found it ironical that Moore could not own his own tissue, and that the University and the biotech companies saw nothing abnormal in their exclusive control of Moore's spleen nor in their patenting of a living organism derived from it. John Moore describes what it's like to be known as Patent No. 4,438,032. 'Without my knowledge or my consent, I was deprived of right of dominion over my own unique genetic material—I was controlled, deceived, lied to and ultimately violated in an unbelievably arrogant and dehumanizing way.'

The US government patent of the Hagahai people was dropped in 1996 as a result of global outrage. This patent was challenged by physicians and activists in Europe, and had to be revoked in 1999. Medical doctors called the patent 'immoral and unethical', and believe that patents such as these are going too far.

For five years between 1994 and 1999, each time the Indian government has introduced WTO-related laws, the patent debate has been the hottest issue in the Indian parliament. Even though the deadline of 1 January 2000 for implementing TRIPs is over, the controversy over patents is still alive and will continue to rage in this millennium. My engagement with the issue of patents and IPRs began in the mid-1980s with the emergence of the new biotechnologies and the patenting of life forms, and the introduction of IPRs in the Uruguay Round of GATT negotiations. My abiding concerns for ecology and equity have been the basis of this engagement with patent laws. As an ecologist dedicated to conservation of biodiversity and reverence for all life, patents on life I believe pose deep ethical problems with far reaching consequences for humanity and other species.

In today's world, patents affect our daily lives—whether we are farmers whose right to save seed is threatened by patents, or we are consumers whose rights to food and medicine are eroded by patent monopolies, or we are researchers whose freedom to exchange knowledge is blocked by patent regimes. And because patents have an impact on every dimension of our everyday lives, we should be active in shaping the patent laws that govern our society. In the first colonization, the land of indigenous people was robbed from them. Through intellectual property rights and patents, the minds and bodies of indigenous people are being pirated; life itself is being colonized. We can thus no longer leave patent issues to patent lawyers and intellectual property experts. I am not a patent lawyer, but my engagement in patent debates over the past decade has been as a scientist, an environmentalist, a feminist and a concerned citizen. This book will I hope demystify patent laws and highlight the ethical, ecological and economic impacts of globalized patent regimes. I hope by the end of this book, the concerns expressed will be yours as well.

The Role of Patents in History

PATENTS ARE ASSOCIATED WITH creativity and invention. They are an exclusive right granted to an inventor to make, produce, distribute and sell the patented product or use patented processes. However, patents have had other functions and meanings in history.

Historically, there are three different uses—'patents for conquests', 'patents for inventions' and 'patents for imports'—to which patents have been put, but the different functions of patents have never been neatly separated in law. Laws are often based on a chaotic mixture of diverse functions because 'patent systems' have been based on what was available historically, and even though they have changed considerably, the change has never been radical enough to cover different socioeconomic contexts, different historical periods and different subject matter. Old legal tools shaped during colonial times have been reshaped with minor adjustments to cover new periods and new domains.

Patents as Instruments of Conquest

The original use of patents had little to do with the present predominant assumption that patents are an effective instrument for stimulating and rewarding inventions and innovations. In the beginning, patents referred to letters patent (a literal translation of the Latin *litterae patents*). The adjective 'patent' means open, and originally patents referred to the 'letters patent' or open letters which were official documents by which certain privileges, rights, ranks or titles were conferred by sovereign rulers. They were 'open' because they were publicly announced and had a seal of the sovereign grantor. The 'openness' had nothing to do with disclosure of an invention as is commonly assumed in the present-day context.

Litterae patents were first issued in Europe in the sixth century. Charters and letters were given by European monarchs for the discovery and conquest of foreign lands on their behalf. They were used for colonization and for establishing import monopolies. This is evident in the charter granted to Christopher Columbus. The most frequent phrase used in the charter was the conjunction of the two verbs 'discover' and 'conquer'. It was used seven times to assert rights to all 'islands and mainlands' before their discovery. Given that Columbus's voyage was supposed to have been to India, and that he landed in the Americas by mistake, it is interesting to reflect on the fact that what Columbus carried as a piece of parchment was the potential right to own India. It was instead used to conquer and own the lands of America's indigenous people who have been called Indians ever since as a reminder of Columbus's mistaken 'discovery'.

Patents have, through history, thus been associated with colonization. At the beginning of the colonization of the world by Europe, they were aimed at conquest of territory; now they are aimed at the conquest of economies. The use of patents as instruments for discovery and conquest has provided the background for the contemporary conflicts over patents generated by GATT/WTO. Patents are often viewed as tools of recolonization by the Third World but are viewed as a 'natural' right, as conquest was during colonialism, by western powers. There are differences of course in yesterday's colonization and today's recolonization. Religion is not the ultimate justification for today's conquest. Recolonization is a 'secular' project, but there is a new religion of the market that drives this so-called secular project. Territory, gold and minerals are no longer the objects of conquest. Markets and economic systems are what have to be controlled. Knowledge itself has to be converted into property, just as land was during colonization. This is why today 'patents' have been covered by the broader label of 'intellectual property' or property in terms of 'products of the mind'. Despite the fact that it was inhabited by indigenous peoples, land that was 'discovered' was treated as '*terra nullius*' or Empty Land because it did not have white European habitation. Similarly, knowledge that is 'invented', 'patented' and converted to 'intellectual property' is often an existing innovation of indigenous knowledge systems. This claim to invention, like the claim to discovery in the patent charters of colonial conquest, is the justification for the take-over of market systems and economic systems through globalized patent regimes. The garb of reward for inventiveness hides the real object—control over the global economy. This secular conquest of diverse knowledge systems and economies is at the heart of the intense conflicts and controversies on patents.

Patents as Rewards for Inventiveness

Patents as 'intellectual property' can be traced to Renaissance Italy, from where they spread to Europe and then to England. In the early period, exploitation of locally unknown devices and processes was rewarded, not new and original inventions.

It was the Venetian Senate which started to differentiate between two kinds of patents—grants of exclusive monopolies which forbade the use of the device without permission while obliging the patent holder to grant licenses to others when 'reasonable' royalties were offered. In March 1474, the Venetian Senate passed the first general patent law which became the historical precedent for stimulating inventions. As the preamble of the Venetian Patent Law states, 'We have among us men of great genius, apt to invent and discover ingenious devices.... Now, if provisions were made for the works and devices discovered by such persons, so that others who may see them could not build them and take the inventors' honour away, more men would then apply their genius, would discover, and would build devices of great utility for our common wealth.' Novelty, however, was defined on the basis of 'new and ingenious' devices not previously made within the Venetian domain. Thus, both imports and inventions were covered. The patent prohibited all private parties except the inventor from making it for ten years. In England, the distinction between 'patents of invention' and 'import patents' was made only in the seventeenth century. Patents of invention were an attempt to free the economy of the abuses of royal grants of monopoly privileges.

Patents as Instruments for Technology Transfer, Catching Up and Import Monopolies

Subsequently, over the past five centuries, patents have been used to transfer existing technologies from technologically advanced countries. Historically, countries which lagged behind in the technology race used patents to 'catch up' with countries technologically more advanced. Technology was 'borrowed' for a specific time period and patents provided monopoly or exclusive rights to the person introducing the invention, giving the person reward and protection. However, in today's context, patents are used as instruments to prevent technology transfer from advanced countries and transfer of knowledge is seen as 'piracy'.

For example, in the fourteenth century, England—later to become the home of the industrial revolution—was in fact a laggard compared to other European countries technologically. In order to catch up, foreign technologies were introduced into England by encouraging the immigration of skilled artisans from abroad. To aid this technological borrowing, patents granted exclusive monopolies and protected these foreign craftsmen while they introduced English apprentices to the 'mysteries' of their arts. Thus, in 1331, Edward II gave letters patent to the Flemish weaver John Kempe. In 1336, two Brabant weavers were encouraged to settle in York. In 1338, three clock makers from Delft were given letters patent in England. Similarly, in 1469, a German, Johann von Speyer, received an exclusive monopoly for the trade of printing in the Venetian domain in exchange for introducing the craft.

Many features of the contemporary patent systems derive from these early roots even though the functions and justifications for granting patents have dramatically changed. The life of patents granted under modern law is one such feature. Since master craftsmen had to train apprentices, they had to reveal the 'mysteries' of their craft. This became the disclosure provision of modern patent systems. Normally it took seven years for an apprentice to learn the art, irrespective of the trade. Hence, the protection was granted for seven or fourteen years, so that at least one or two generations of trainees could be technologically trained. The patent, giving a monopoly of the trade during the period of training, granted the instructors protection from competition by their students. After the expiry of the patent or privilege, trained apprentices could practice the art whose 'mysteries' they had learned. The life of patents for seven or fourteen years is then linked to this use of patents as incentives for training.

Another feature is that of granting patents based on 'originality' merely in the country into which the knowledge is being introduced and not necessarily on 'absolute novelty'. Thus, while many of the innovations of the industrial revolution were made in Europe, originality of the process or invention in England alone was sufficient basis for granting a patent in England. Patents were granted to 'inventors' such as James Rumsey who had never built a boat, but who was granted the exclusive monopoly to navigate rivers. John Fitch was granted a patent in the US state of Pennsylvania on 28 March 1787 which gave him the 'sole and exclusive right and privilege of constructing, making, using, employing and navigating all and every species or kinds of boats or water crafts…in all creeks, rivers, nays and waters whatsoever, within the territory and jurisdiction of this state [Pennsylvania], for and during the full term of fourteen years' (Fred Warshofsky, *Patent Wars*, 1994). Thus, broad steamboat patents to make, use and navigate all and every species of steamboats were granted in the US in spite of the steam engine having been invented and patented by James Watt in Scotland in 1772!

Patent laws were framed to encourage such technology transfer and commercialization. The US became the first modern nation state to enact such patent laws—first at the state (or as they were then known, colony) level, and later, after independence, at the federal level. As in England, encouragement of technology transfer, rather than prevention of technology transfer, was the basis of the patents granted in the US. The early US patent laws, like European laws, were for introducing new methods which were unknown in the US, but practised elsewhere. They were not related to inventiveness, only to the fact that the practice was not being undertaken within the US and hence could be treated as 'presumed to be unknown'. Present-day states in the US started to pass laws to protect monopolies, often based on use of imported technologies and methods of manufacture. Salt patents were among the first to be granted in the colonies. For example, in 1641, Samuel Winslow was granted an exclusive right to make salt.

Patents acquired the objective of promoting manufacture, not rewarding invention. The US, which depended on borrowed knowledge for its own development of industrial power, a century later, wanted any similar transfer of knowledge and technology to be blocked.

Two elements have had critical influence in shaping US laws and hence in shaping global laws. The first is the myth of 'discovery' that goes hand-in-hand with the original definition of the scope of letters patent that allowed it to be said that Columbus 'discovered' America. The second is the myth of 'ignorance as innovation'. For example, if somebody in Europe were operating a machine and someone in the US independently and without knowledge of that existence in good faith developed his/her own invention, which was essentially the same machine, the fact that the a similar machine was already operating in Europe would not prevent him/her from obtaining a patent in the US. The European invention would not be considered *prior art* in US law. This is categorically stated in the Connecticut law which treats invention as 'bringing in the supply of goods from foreign parts, that is not as yet of use among us.'

Originally, the US federal laws were a patchwork of state

laws and did not offer protection for the patentee outside the state in which it had been granted. The national statute was institutionalized in 1787. The assumption of 'ignorance of invention' is enshrined in the US Patent Act of 1952. Section 102 of the Act talks of *use in the US*, not use in foreign countries, as *prior art*. The US Patent Act, which was designed to make the country an independent industrial power, was thus deliberately designed to deny *prior art* and hence treat ignorance of prior innovation as the grounds for invention. *Prior art* and *prior use* in other countries has thus been systematically ignored in US laws when granting monopolies on the basis of claims to invention. Since US-style patent laws are designed to grant patents for new inventions based on denial or non-recognition of *prior art* elsewhere, they allow patents to be granted for existing knowledge. This is the basis of biopiracy. Paradoxically then, a legal system aimed at preventing 'intellectual piracy' is itself based on legitimizing piracy.

Patents and Control Over the Global Economy

Today, land and gold have given way to knowledge as the wealth of nations. Property in factories, minerals, real estate and gold is being rapidly replaced by property in products of the mind or 'intellectual property'. Patents which refer to knowledge as 'property' remain an instrument of colonization. While colonial wars of the past were fought over geographical territory, colonization today is based on wars over intellectual territory.

Two major shifts led to the emergence of patents or 'intellectual property' as central to the reorganization of economic systems. These changes in the scope, meaning and implications of patents and patent laws have in turn engendered conflicts between countries, between governments and the public, and between corporations and citizens.

Firstly, the imperatives of economic growth and capital accumulation led industrialized countries to search for global markets. They have therefore sought to secure global market access through free trade agreements such as the Uruguay Round of GATT, now embodied in the rules of WTO. Secondly, leading industrialized countries like the US have seen a decline in their manufacture as other countries have taken the lead. In the 1980s, the trade deficit of the US was $150 billion. The supremacy of the US was threatened by competition from Japan and other newly industrializing countries. The US therefore decided to maintain its supremacy by making intellectual property and patents its primary asset for economic growth, for control of world trade and capture of international markets.

Patents have become the most important asset of the US and a growing component of exports. In 1947, intellectual property comprised just under ten per cent of all US exports. In 1986, the figure had grown to thirty-seven per cent and by 1994 it was well over fifty per cent.

But trade in knowledge as property could only take place if all countries could be forced to recognize this form of property and frame intellectual property laws on the lines of US law. In 1987, the US computer software and pharmaceutical industries lobbied with the US administration under Reagan to assess the increased markets US commerce could control if other countries had the same laws as the US. These potential markets were treated as a national loss to the US economy due to other countries having different patent laws from the US. The US International Trade Commission calculated the 'losses' to be $ 43–61 billion every year. If every country could be forced to have US-style patent laws, the US trade deficit could be substantially reduced.

This is how intellectual property was brought to GATT and the TRIPs of the WTO became the framework for patent laws globally. Global implementation of US laws on patents and intellectual property became the agenda of western powers. This agenda was also linked to shifts taking place in terms of technology. In place of machines and molecules, the new inventions driving technological and economic growth were in the areas of information technology and biotechnology.

Patents on machines and chemicals had also been surrounded by conflicts between rights of business and rights of the public. But patents on life forms triggered by biotechnology have generated new conflicts related to ethical questions and ecological and economic impacts. Patents on products and processes derived from biological resources and living organisms also raise questions about who is the pirate and who is the innovator since very often what is being patented is indigenous knowledge and traditional innovation. Further, as the fossil fuel era gives way to the age of biology, patents on living material become the means of controlling both the raw material and the markets of the Third World.

The Myth of Patents

The Myth of Stimulating Creativity

THE MYTH THAT PATENTS contribute to the stimulation of creativity and inventiveness and their absence to lack of creativity and ingenuity is based on an artificial construction of knowledge and innovation—that of knowledge being isolated in time and space, without being connected to the social fabric and contributions from the past. Based on this construct, knowledge is thus seen as capital, a commodity and as a means for exclusive market control. As capital, it gives the owner a competitive edge, as commodity the patented information is sold and franchised to others on terms that are often onerous, and as an instrument of exclusive market control, the 'patent' ensures that no one can enter, or even manufacture, in that market. In these ways, patents enforce dominant and exclusive control.

Knowledge, however, by its very nature is a collective, cumulative enterprise. It is based on exchange within a community. It is an expression of human creativity; both individual and collective. Since creativity has diverse expressions, science is a pluralistic enterprise which refers to different 'ways of knowing'. The term 'science' cannot be used to refer only to modern western science. It should include the knowledge systems of diverse cultures in different periods of history. But patents are granted for private intellectual property, built on the fiction of totally individualistic scientific innovation. There is then an intrinsic conflict built into the granting of patents as private rights for individual innovation and creativity and the view of knowledge as a collective endeavour.

Recent work in the history, philosophy and sociology of science has revealed that scientists do not work in accordance with an abstract scientific method, putting forward theories based on direct and neutral observation. Modern science does not leave us with any criteria that distinguish the theoretical claims of modern western science from those of indigenous non-western sciences. And although the totally artificial Cartesian construction of a disembodied mind generating knowledge was given up a century ago, it is still the model on which patent regimes are based.

Recognition of diverse traditions of creativity is an essential component of keeping diverse knowledge systems alive. This is particularly important in this period of rampant ecological destruction in which the smallest source of ecological knowledge and insights can become a vital link to the future of humanity. Indigenous knowledge systems are by and large ecological, while the dominant model of scientific knowledge, characterized by reductionism and fragmentation, is not equipped to take the complexity of interrelations in nature fully into account. This inadequacy becomes most significant in the domain of life sciences which deals with living organisms. Creativity in the life sciences has to include the following three levels:

1. The creativity inherent to living organisms which allows them to evolve, recreate and regenerate themselves.
2. The creativity of the knowledge systems of indigenous communities who have learnt how to conserve and utilize the rich biological diversity of our planet.

3. The creativity of modern scientists in university or corporate labs, who find ways to use living organisms to generate profits.

The recognition of these diverse creativities is essential for the conservation of biodiversity as well as for the conservation of intellectual diversity—across cultures, and within the private and public research setting.

Even though many of the patents being claimed in the US are based on Third World biodiversity and Third World knowledge, it is falsely assumed that without IPR protection, creativity lies buried. Western powers view human creativity as a vast national resource and believe it will remain buried without encouragement for extraction, like minerals under the earth. According to them, intellectual property protection is the tool which releases that resource.

This interpretation of creativity, as unleashed only when formal regimes of IPR protection are in place, is a total negation of creativity in nature and creativity generated by non-profit motives in both industrial and non-industrial societies. It is a denial of the role of innovation in traditional cultures, as well as in the public domain. In fact, the dominant interpretation of IPRs leads to a dramatic distortion in the understanding of creativity and, as a result, in the understanding of the history of inequality and poverty.

The economic inequality between the affluent industrialized countries and the poor Third World countries is a product of 500 years of colonialism, and the continued maintenance and creation of mechanisms for draining wealth out of the Third World. According to the United Nations Development Programme, while $50 billion flows annually from the North to the South in terms of aid, the South loses $500 billion every year in terms of interest payments on debt and loss of fair prices for commodities due to unequal terms of trade.

Instead of seeing the structural inequality of the international economic system as lying at the roots of Third World poverty, IPR advocates explain poverty as arising from lack of creativity, which in turn is seen as rooted in the lack of IPR protection. They then put in place systems which will further drain wealth from the poor to the rich, the South to the North.

For example, Robert Sherwood in his book *Intellectual Property and Economic Development* relates two stories, one real and one quite imaginary. In his words, they are meant to draw a contrast between the mindset of ordinary people in a non-protection country and in a country with effective protection:

> A salesman for a US pump manufacturer, who was a neighbour of the author some years ago in upstate New York, noticed while visiting customers that a certain type of pressure valve would be useful. Although his wife was sceptical, he took time at night and weekends to design such a valve and applied for and was granted a patent on the design. He placed a second mortgage on his house and later obtained a bank loan, largely on the strength of the patent. He created a small business, employed a dozen people and contributed to the multiplier effect before the valve was superceded some 20 years later by other types of valves. The man never thought much about intellectual property. He simply took for granted that he could get a patent and build a business from it.
>
> In Lima, Peru, young Carlos (a fictional proxy for much of the developing world) earns a meager living welding replacement mufflers under trucks and cars. He thinks of a clamp for simplified muffler installation. His wife is sceptical. Should he spend his nights and

weekends to design and develop the clamp? He will need help fabricating a prototype. Should he involve his friend, the metal worker? He needs money for metal and tools. Should he use the money saved under the mattress? Should he take a bus across town to ask his sister's husband for a loan? The answer to each question is strongly biased towards the negative by weak intellectual property protection. Without thinking much about intellectual property, his wife, the brother-in-law and Carlos himself each knows from community wisdom that his idea is vulnerable and likely to be taken by others. He cannot take for granted that his idea can be protected. In this story, lack of confidence that his idea can be protected would in all probability lead Carlos to a negative decision at each of these decision points.

If the story of Carlos is multiplied many times across a landscape, that country's opportunity loss is devastating. When an effective protection system becomes a reality, confidence grows that intellectual assets are valuable and protectable. Then the inventive and creative habit of mind, which is at the heart of an intellectual property protection system, will spread in the minds of people.

Central to the ideology of IPRs is this fallacy, recounted above, that people are creative only if they can make profits and such profits are guaranteed through IPR protection. This negates the scientific creativity of those not spurred by the search for profits, i.e., the majority of scientists in universities and public research systems. It negates the creativity of traditional societies and the modern scientific community in which free exchange of ideas is the very condition for creativity, not its anti-thesis. Global patent regimes are however more closely linked with the import monopolies for which the original patent systems were designed, than with the 'reward for creativity' argument used to justify patents.

The Myth of Technology Transfer, Innovation and R&D

The argument frequently promoted for a uniform worldwide IPR system is that such a system will promote investment research and technology transfer in developing countries. The 'disclosure' clauses in patent laws which are related to medieval incentives for 'revealing the mysteries of the art' are now conveniently projected as necessary for the transferring of knowledge to society. However, the opposite is true. When companies can import products under import monopolies granted by patents, they have no incentive to set up domestic manufacture, or set up local R&D, or transfer technology for local production.

Stronger patent protection also does not automatically translate into higher innovation or more investment in R&D, and not all sectors of industry have innovations connected to patent protection. Edwin Mansfield (1990) has shown that in the US, based on a random sample of 100 firms from twelve industries, patent protection was judged to be essential for the development or introduction of 50 per cent or more of the inventions in only two industries—pharmaceuticals and chemicals. In another three industries (petroleum, machinery and fabricated metal products), 10–20 per cent of the inventions were dependent on patent protection. In other sectors, patent protection had no impact on innovation.

The World Bank's *World Development Report 1998–99* examined the experience of more than eighty countries and found that the effect of intellectual property rights on trade flows in high-tech goods was insignificant. *The Human Development*

Project Report, 1999 of the UNDP also indicates that tighter intellectual property rights do not spur multinationals to carry out in-country research and development. IPR systems are in fact inducing a shift from the public domain to the private domain, and from the South to the North. R&D in the South has dropped from 6 per cent in the mid-1980s to 4 per cent in the mid-1990s. The portion of public sector patents in bio-technology sold under exclusive license to the private sector has risen from just 6 per cent in 1981 to more than 40 per cent in 1990.

The privatization of research has not led to competition but consolidation. Pharmaceutical, food, chemical, cosmetics, energy and seed industries are combining to form giant life-sciences corporations. In 1998, the top ten companies in each industry controlled 32 per cent of the $23 billion seed industry, 35 per cent of the $297 billion pharmaceutical industry, 60 per cent of the $17 billion veterinary medicine industry, and 85 per cent of the $31 billion pesticide industry.

Concentration is not just at the level of corporations but also at the level of countries. Industrial countries hold 97 per cent of all patents worldwide. In 1995, the US alone collected half the royalty fees in the world. Just ten countries have 95 per cent of the US patents and capture 90 per cent of the cross-border royalties and licensing fees, and 70 per cent of the global royalty and licensing for payments were between parent and affiliate multinational corporations. The top fifty corporations own over a quarter of all patents in the US. In USA and Germany, 12 per cent of R&D came from companies; in Europe 81 per cent of all Swiss R&D expenditure and 69 per cent of Dutch R&D was accounted for by four firms.

Trends in International Transfer of Technology in Developing Countries, a 1985 study conducted by UNCTAD which covered 100 corporations, found the role of patents vis-a-vis innovation was not only sector specific, but that it also differed on a country-to-country basis. There is no uniform cross-sectoral link between IPRs and innovation. Even in sectors where IPRs do play a role, they produce some particularly unhealthy side-effects. A recent study by Michael Kremer (1996) reaffirms the heavily distorted relationship between the drug industry and the patent system, where the IPR incentive works to increase prices and lower consumption.

It is also often argued that patents are a legitimate system for corporations to recoup investment made on R&D. However, corporations usually buy up patents from small inventors or from public sector institutions or, in the case of biopiracy patents, from traditional societies. For example, 92 per cent of cancer drugs discovered between 1955 and 1992 were developed with funding from the US government, but patents for cancer drugs are owned by MNCs. Further, patent monopolies have always been claimed in the name of the poor inventor whose creativity in virtually all cases has been absorbed or cheaply bought out by mighty enterprises.

In 1996, the US earned $30 billion from royalties and licenses. On the other hand, the South spent $18 billion for buying patented technology in 1995. In certain cases, companies do not sell the technology in order to maintain a monopoly. This happened to India in the case of alternatives to CFCs, which were banned under the Montreal Protocol because they destroy the ozone layer. The US corporation which has patents on the alternatives to CFCs refused to license the technology to India. In 1996, the level of MNC investments in foreign affiliates had reached $1.4 trillion. Of the technology transfers through royalty payments and licensing fees,

70 per cent occurs between parent companies and their foreign affiliates.

Third World countries are losing their technological capacities, while global corporations are keeping tight control over patented technologies even when they move across borders. The global patent regime as determined by the TRIPs agreement is making the Third World lose twice over on the technology transfer front. First, indigenous technology is being pirated and patented through IPR systems. A UNDP study shows that Third World countries are losing $300 million in unpaid royalties for farmers' seeds and over $5 billion in unpaid royalties for medicinal plants, if 2 per cent royalty was charged on biological diversity developed by Third World communities. Instead of paying the South what it is owed for use of indigenous knowledge, the US is claiming that the South owes $202 million for agrichemicals royalties and $2.5 billion for pharmaceutical royalties, which is the figure calculated on the assumption that the Third World is introducing US-style patent laws.

Patent systems are therefore a drain of technology and wealth from the South to the North, not a mechanism for technology transfer from rich countries to poor countries. As countries are forced to implement TRIPs, the outflow of scarce foreign exchange for royalty payments will add to the debt burden, pushing poor countries deeper into poverty, especially since the TRIPs agreement is expanding patents to food and agriculture, seeds and plants. Third World resources and knowledge are thus being converted into the 'intellectual property' of northern corporations, which will collect royalties from Third World countries similar to the time when colonizers took resources from them in the first instance.

The Myth of Knowledge Generation

Without patents, it is said, knowledge will stay secret. There are three flaws in this argument. Firstly, in the absence of patents, knowledge is shared, not kept secret. Secondly, what is provided through patents is not knowledge, but information, and since patents prevent others from using that information during the life of the patent, making the information public is not useful. Finally, patents have been known to prevent transfer of technology between the North and the South. Patents are thus primarily a means of generating revenue, not for generating or transferring knowledge.

Institutions of learning and knowledge generation have been based on the free flow of knowledge in classrooms, journals and books. This free flow is now being blocked. Universities are being transformed from centres of learning and research, producing knowledge as a service to the public, to centres for the production of knowledge as intellectual property. Most research knowledge, evolution and innovation has taken place in the public domain without patent protection because human beings respond to many sources of incentives. When citations and publications are the main incentive, scientists have worked on the logic of 'publish or perish'. With the changes induced in the research culture by IPR systems, the logic is becoming 'patent or perish'. However, the secrecy necessary for nurturing a patent culture will kill the openness required for nurturing a knowledge culture. Since knowledge is a social product, undermining the social fabric of knowledge generation and innovation will undermine its generation and transfer.

An argument often made is that without IPRs there will be no incentive for research. But IPRs are changing the incentive system, from serving the public good to working for private gain. The knowledge community is giving way to the corporate university. Thus, a privately funded centre at MIT hires one-third of the biologists on the faculty and thereby owns all the intellectual property they create.

Wherever patents have been associated with scientific research, the result has been closure of communication. While scientists have never been as open as popular mythology portrays, the threat to scientific communication posed by scientists working with commercial enterprises is becoming a major cause for concern. As Emmanuel Epstein, a noted microbiologist, states: 'In the past it was the most natural thing in the world for colleagues to swap ideas on the spur of the moment, to share the latest findings hot off the scintillation counter or the electrophoresis cell, to show each other early drafts of papers, and in other such ways to act as companions in zealous research. [But], no more' (quoted in Martin Kenney, *Biotechnology: The University-Industrial Complex*).

Reflecting on the closure of scientific openness in the University Industrial Complex, Martin Kenny (1993) observes 'that the fear of being scooped or of seeing one's work transformed into a commodity can silence those who presumably are colleagues. To see a thing that one produced turned into a product for sale by someone over whom one has no control can leave a person feeling violated. The labour of love is converted into a plain commodity—the work now is an item to be exchanged on the basis of its market price. Money becomes the arbiter of a scientific development's value.'

Openness, the free exchange of ideas and information, and the free exchange of materials and techniques have been critical components in the creativity and productivity of the research community. By introducing secrecy in science, IPRs and the associated commercialization and privatization of knowledge will kill the scientific community, and hence its potential for creativity. IPRs exploit creativity, while killing its very source. We know that reservoirs that are not replenished soon run dry. Commons sense tells us that when roots of a tree are not nourished, it dies. Not only do patents have the potential of destroying knowledge, they also destroy productive capacity and undermine the potential for development.

Independence from economic interest has been the hall-mark of knowledge institutions. Corporatisation is however transforming the nature of knowledge itself as commercial ties start to shape the research agenda and commercially-biased private interest knowledge displaces public interest knowledge. Sheldon Krimsky in his book *Biotechnics and Society: The Rise of Industrial Genetics* points to a study of publications in fourteen leading science and medical journals by scientists from Massachusetts in 1992. The study found that more than one-third of the authors had a financial interest in their research, 20 per cent were linked to the biotechnology industry and 22 per cent had applied for a patent related to the subject of the article.

Corporate sponsored research can create biased research, as has been shown by many studies, inordinately favouring corporate sponsors and undermining the public interest. Not only does the public interest disappear in research in corporate and IPR dominated systems, entire disciplines are erased as commercialization becomes the yardstick for assessing the relevance of teaching and research programmes. Once priorities shift from social need to potential return on investment, which is the main criterion for commercially guided research, entire streams of knowledge and learning will be forgotten and will go extinct. While these diverse fields might not be commercially profitable, they are socially necessary. For example, we need epidemiology, ecology, and evolutionary and developmental biology as a society facing ecological problems. We need experts on particular taxonomic groups such as microbes, insects and plants to respond to the crisis of biodiversity erosion. The moment we ignore the useful and necessary and concentrate only on the profitable, we are destroying the social conditions for the creation of intellectual diversity. The ultimate logic of the privatization of knowledge is to define free exchange of knowledge as theft and priacy. Unfortunately, the criminalization of knowledge exchange is already a reality.

Of Spies, Crime and IPRs

Imperial power has always been based on a convergence of military power used in the defence of trade. This convergence was at the heart of the gunboat diplomacy during colonialism. A similar convergence is now taking shape around the defence of trading interests in a period of globalization and so-called free trade. This can be seen in the legislation passed by the US Congress in 1996 which views IPRs as vital to national security. It can be interpreted as criminalizing the natural development and exchange of knowledge as it empowers US intelligence agencies to investigate the activities of ordinary persons worldwide in an effort to protect the intellectual property rights of US corporations. Increasing the absurdity of this action is our awareness that what is seen as 'intellectual property' is often information 'pirated' from non-western societies and indigenous communities.

The British empire was built through the destruction of manufacturing capacities in the colonies and the prevention of the emergence of such capacity. 'Free trade' during the era of the 'technological superiority' of England was based on the thumbs of master weavers in Bengal being cut off, the forced cultivation of indigo by the peasants of Bihar, the slave trade from Africa to supply free labour to cotton plantations in the US and the extermination of the indigenous people of North America. It also included laws that prevented technology transfer. From 1765 to 1789, the English parliament passed a series of strict laws preventing the export of new machines, or plans, or models of them. Skilled people who worked the machines were not allowed to leave England to ensure that England remained the industrial power.

Samuel Slater, who is called the 'Father of American Manufacture' acted in violation of these British laws when he came to the US secretly carrying the knowledge of mechanical spinning and weaving from England to the US. He transferred his experience of working in the English factories to the US and built the first complete mill for spinning yarn. While the US built its economic power and manufacturing capacity by breaking free of British monopolies, the current US Congress and present day corporations appear unwilling to allow this spirit of freedom, so fundamental to US history/economic development, to exist anywhere in the world.

Anyone following the steps of Samuel Slater today would be arrested for 15 years or fined up to $10 million under a new Act called the Economic Espionage Act of 1996 in the US. The Economic Espionage Act takes espionage from military domains to economic domains, it redefines intellectual property infringement as a crime, and justifies the use of intelligence agencies to deal with issues of science and technology exchange. As the introduction of the Act states: 'There can be no question that the development of propriety economic information is an integral part of America's economic well-being. Moreover, the nation's economic interests are a part of its national security interests. Thus threats to the nation's economic interest are threats to the nation's vital security interests'. Transfer of technology has, through the Act, been redefined as 'economic or industrial espionage'.

While it cannot be denied that every country has a right to protect its national security, there are, however, problems with the Economic Espionage Act. Firstly, it is defining the 'nation's economic interest' as the 'nation's security interest' in a period of globalization and trade liberalization and hence uses the arguments of national security asymmetrically. Globalization is being used to force other countries to give up their national interest, national security and national sovereignty. Thus, the US has taken India to the WTO because India's parliament was acting in its national interest when it prevented the amendment of the Indian Patent Act. The US also uses the Super 301 and the Special 301 clauses of its trade act to force countries to undermine their national security in order to create opportunities for US corporations. Similarly, the US is forcing Europe to import a herbicide resistant genetically engineered soyabean manufactured by a major US corporation in spite of consumer resistance to genetically engineered foods. While denying other countries their national security and sovereignty, The US is using the reinterpretation of national security to increase the global control of US corporations over resources, technology and markets. The Economic Espionage Act shows that contrary to the dominant idea that globalization implies an end of the nation-state, the state is alive and well and in the active service of MNCs in the US!

Secondly, the definition of economic espionage in terms of intellectual property infringement is arbitrary and biased, especially since intellectual property is being expanded into new areas. This includes the public domain of university systems as well as the collective knowledge heritage of non-western societies. The move to privatize the public domain and the intellectual commons through IPRs is in itself a 'theft' of knowledge. The introduction of the Economic Espionage Act in the context of biopiracy and intellectual piracy gives to the US corporations and intelligence agencies a dangerous tool which can be used against the general public and ordinary scientists.

The dangers of arbitrary action through the Economic Espionage Act can be illustrated by the case of a student, Peter Taborsky, who was arrested, sentenced to prison, and fined $20,000 for 'stealing' his own idea. (Although this case involves US domestic law rather than international law/trade agreements, one can imagine similar injustices occurring anywhere in the global picture of US economic involvement.) Peter Taborsky worked as a lab assistant in the University of Florida on a project funded by Progressive Technologies Corporation. Outside his scheduled work hours Peter did his own research for which he obtained a patent. He was accused of 'theft' by the University and the Corporation because he had used the lab and equipment. Peter's arrest dramatizes the problems of IPRs linked to private funding of public institutions. Most labs and research facilities have been built by public funds. When a corporation finances a project and the research product becomes its intellectual property, it is forgotten that the facilities that make knowledge production possible were built up as a public resource. Later, when someone uses that public resource to generate new ideas it is treated as theft, as in the case of Peter Taborsky.

Under the US Espionage Act, a researcher like Peter would

be liable for a fine of up to $10 million instead of $20,000 and a sentence of fourteen years instead of one year.

Scientific and technological development depends on the free exchange of knowledge, technologies and ideas; now such exchange is being defined as espionage. The absurdity of 'intellectual property theft' becomes even more dramatic in cases where 'intellectual property' is derived from the transfer of knowledge from non-western and indigenous systems to western corporations. The Espionage Act, in a world characterized by biopiracy, carries the danger of transforming the everyday activities of farmers and healers, students and researchers, scientists and industrialists into crime and espionage. US corporations have 'pirated' indigenous innovations and claimed it as their 'intellectual property'. Examples include patents on *neem*, *haldi* and *Phyllanthus niruri*. Will the intelligence agencies of the US government be used to protect this 'intellectual property'? What methods will be used to destabilize the traditional uses, lifestyles and cultures in order to protect 'the owners of proprietary economic information' such as W.R. Grace which owns the majority of *neem* patents. What would happen if Third World countries used the same logic as the US and declared all bioprospectors and ethnobotanists working for US corporations as engaged in 'economic espionage' and a threat to 'national security'?

There are seven categories of intellectual property or 'property in the products of the mind' that are covered by the TRIPs agrreement. These include:

1. Patents
2. Industrial design
3. Trademarks
4. Geographical Indications or Appellations of origin
5. Layout designs (topographies) of integrated circuits

6. Undisclosed information or trade secrets
7. Copyrights, covering literary, artistic, musical, photographic and audio visual works.

In the popular perception, all the different forms of IPRs are equated with patents though patents are one form of IPRs. Economically, patents are the most significant since they have the maximum impact on basic needs and livelihood and the structure of the economy. Patents are also the strongest form of IPR protection.

However, the 'reward for creativity' and the 'return on investment' argument in favour of patents is flawed. Patents have become the right of capital to control markets. This is the reason patent laws like India's 1970 Patent Act put a limit on the monopoly profits that corporations can derive from the commercialization of a technology. Exclusions from patentability is a strategy for limits on monopolies. Methods of horticulture and agriculture, as well as food, have been excluded in the Indian patent law because 75 per cent of the people are dependent on agriculture as a livelihood, and because so many people are poor, that even their entitlement for food is limited. Similarly, drugs and medicines have been excluded because millions do not have access to health care, and costly medicines would take health care even further beyond the reach of people. If food and medicine are available only at a price that is beyond the reach of people, the basic promise of the patent system as a contract that encourages private gain so that public goods can be provided is undermined. When the consumer's rights to food and health are undermined, there is no ground for granting patents, since patents are supposed to be a balance between the interests of producers on the one hand and consumers on the other, i.e., those who develop or commercialize a technological innovation and those who use the goods and services derived from it.

The globalization of western-style IPR systems, in a world of deep inequalities, is a direct assault on the economic rights of the poor. As Deepak Nayyar has observed, 'It is essential to ensure rewards for innovators, but surely the protection of monopoly profits should not take precedence over the interests of consumers in a world characterized by uneven development'. The challenge is to strike a balance—enough protection to encourage innovation, but not so much that the social good is not served. The TRIPs agreement unfortunately has gone overboard in protecting investors' rights, but has not gone far enough to create a regime for protection of the public interest.

Threats to Biodiversity

WHILE PATENTS HAVE HAD different meanings and functions through history, during the 20th century they have been associated with inventions of new machines and molecules, which are clearly manmade artifacts. Patents on machines and molecules reflected the two industrial revolutions related to mechanical engineering and chemical engineering. There is, however, a new industrial revolution under way in the form of genetic engineering—the manipulation and engineering of life forms at the genetic level. There is therefore an attempt to expand patents to cover life forms or biodiversity— the ecological term that refers to the diversity of life forms.

The first step taken to patent life was in the case of a genetically engineered micro-organism. Prior to 1980, the US Patent and Trademark Office interpreted the US Patent Law, with some notable exceptions, as not intended to cover living things such as laboratory created micro-organisms. On 16 June 1980, however, the United States Supreme Court ruled in Diamond, Commissioner of Patents and Trademarks vs Chakravarty that a new manmade micro-organism that could break down oil was patentable subject matter because it comprised a manufacture or composition of matter.

The story goes as follows. In 1980, General Electric and one of its employees, Ananda Mohan Chakravarty, applied for a patent on a genetically-engineered bacteria. Essentially all that was done was simply shuffling genes, changing bacteria that already existed. While Chakravarty did not claim to have 'created' life, the United States Supreme Court interpreted genetic engineering of the micro-organism as 'manufacture'. Chakravarty was granted his patent on the grounds that the micro-organism was not a product of nature but his own invention and therefore patentable. As Andrew Kimbrell, a leading US lawyer recounts, 'In coming to its precedent shattering decision, the court seemed unaware that the inventor himself had characterized his "creation" of the microbe as simply "shuffling genes, not creating life"'. Thus it was on such slippery grounds that the first patent on life was granted and in spite of exclusion of plants and animals in US Patent Law, the US has since then rushed on to grant patents on all kinds of life forms.

When it comes to life forms, genetic scientists have gotten away with the claim that they have 'invented' and 'made' the living organism into which they have introduced a new gene and hence can claim it as their patented property, with the right to exclude others from 'making' it, using it and selling it, unless they pay royalties to the patent owner. Currently, hundreds of genetically engineered animals, including fish, cows, mice and pigs are figuratively standing in line to be patented by a variety of researchers and corporations. The patenting of microbes is leading inexorably to the patenting of plants, and then animals.

Biodiversity has been redefined as 'biotechnological inventions' and 'gene constructs' to make the patenting of life forms appear less controversial. These patents are valid for twenty years and hence cover future generations of plants and animals. However, even when scientists in universities or corporations shuffle genes, they do not 'create' the organism which they patent. Referring to the landmark Chakravarty case in the US many scientists believe that Chakravarty did not create a new form of life; he merely intervened in the normal processes by which strains of bacteria exchange genetic information to produce a new strain. 'His' bacterium lives and reproduces itself under the forces that guide all cellular life. We are thus far, far away from being able to create life. The argument that the bacterium is Chakravarty's handiwork and not nature's wildly exaggerates human power and displays an ignorance of biology, and this has had such devastating impact on the ecology of our planet.

Patents on life and the positioning of man as an inventor of other beings have tremendous economic and ecological implications, apart from ethical problems. Life forms 'make' themselves—they grow, reproduce, regenerate and multiply through their intrinsic complex and dynamic structures. Manipulation of life forms is not equal to 'making' life. Introducing genes into life forms is not the same as 'making' life. Patents on life amount to claiming the role of Creator or God. Once patenting of biodiveristy, its genes, cells, processes and products become possible, it is an easy step to move beyond patents on genetically engineered organisms and start claiming patents on plants.

Ecologically, patents related to biological resources have major implications for the conservation of biodiversity and its sustainable use. By creating 'property' in life through patents, the economically powerful corporations can become the new 'life-lords', just as earlier we had landlords or *zamindars*. They can collect rent for every seed sown, every medicine made from the free gifts of nature's biodiversity which have been freely accessible to people for generations. The giving of the power to collect 'rents from life' through patents is a guaranteed means of pushing millions to the edge of survival.

Columbus set the precedence in treating the license to conquer non-European peoples as a *natural right* of European men. The colonizers' freedom was built on the slavery and subjugation of the people with original rights to the land. This violent takeover was rendered 'natural' by defining the colonized people into nature, thus denying them their humanity and freedom. Locke's treatise on property effectively legitimized this same process of theft and robbery during the enclosure movement in Europe. Locke clearly articulates capitalism's freedom to build on the freedom to steal; he states that property is created by removing resources from nature. According to Locke, only capital can add value to appropriated nature, and hence only those who own the capital have the natural right to own natural resources; a right that supersedes the common rights of others with prior claims. Capital is thus defined as a source of freedom, but this freedom is based on the denial of freedom to the land, forests, rivers and biodiversity that capital claims as its own. Because property obtained through privatization of the commons is equated with freedom, those commoners laying claim to it are perceived to be depriving the owners of capital of their freedom. Thus, peasants and tribals who demand the return of their rights and access to resources are regarded as thieves and saboteurs.

The take over of territories and land in the past, and the takeover of biodiversity and indigenous knowledge now, is based on 'emptying' land and biodiversity of all relationships to indigenous people. All sustainable cultures, in their diversity, have viewed the earth as *terra mater* (mother earth). The colonial construct of the passivity of the earth and the consequent creation of the colonial category of land as *terra nullius* (empty land) served two purposes—it denied the existence and prior rights of original inhabitants and negated the regenerative capacity and life processes of the earth. In the case of Australia, the concept of *terra nullius* was used to justify the appropriation of land and its natural resources by declaring the entire continent uninhabited. This declaration enabled the colonizers to privatize the commons relatively easily, because as far as they were concerned, there were no commons existing in the first place!

The eurocentric concept of property views only capital investment as investment, and hence treats returns on capital investment as the only right that needs protection. Non-western indigenous communities and cultures recognize that investment can also be of labour or of care and nurturance. Rights in such cultural systems protect investments beyond capital. They protect the culture of conservation and the culture of caring and sharing.

There are major differences between ownership of resources shaped in Europe during the enclosures movement and during colonial take over, and 'ownership' as it has been practised by tribals and farmers throughout history across diverse societies. The former is based on ownership as private property, based on concepts of returns on investment for profits. The latter is based on entitlements through usufruct rights, based on concepts of return on labour to provide for ourselves, our children, our families, our communities. Usufruct rights can be privately held or held in common. When held in common, they define common property.

The Enclosure of the Commons

The 'enclosure' of biodiversity and knowledge is the final step in a series of enclosures that began with the rise of colonialism. Land and forests were the first resources to be 'enclosed' and converted from commons to commodities. Later, water resources were 'enclosed' through dams, groundwater mining and privatization schemes. Now it is the turn of biodiversity and knowledge to be 'enclosed' through IPRs.

In the globalization era, the commons are being enclosed and the power of communities is being undermined by a corporate enclosure in which life itself is being transformed into the private property of corporations. The corporate enclosure is happening in two ways. Firstly, IPR systems are allowing the 'enclosure' of biodiversity and knowledge, thus eroding the commons and the community. Secondly, the corporation is being treated as the only form of association with a legal personality.

The destruction of the commons was essential for the industrial revolution, to provide a supply of raw material to industry. A life-support system can be shared, it cannot be owned as private property or exploited for private profit. The commons, therefore, had to be privatized, and people's sustenance base in these commons had to be appropriated, to feed the engine of industrial progress and capital accumulation. The enclosure of the commons has been called the revolution of the rich against the poor. However, enclosures are not just a historical episode that occurred during the sixteenth century in England. The enclosure of the commons can be a guiding metaphor for understanding the conflicts being generated by the expansion of IPR systems to biodiversity.

The policy of deforestation and the enclosure of the commons which started in England, was later replicated in the colonies like India. The first Indian Forest Act was passed in 1865 by the Supreme Legislative Council, which authorized the government to declare forests and wastelands (*benap* or 'unmeasured lands') as reserved forests. The introduction of this legislation marks the beginning of what is called the 'scientific management' of forests. It basically mounted to the formalization of the erosion of forests and of the rights of local people to forest produce. Though the forests were converted into state property, forest reservation was in fact an enclosure because it converted a common resource into a commercial one. The state merely mediated in the privatization.

In the colonial period, peasants were forced to grow indigo instead of food, salt was taxed to provide revenues for the British military, and meanwhile, forests were being enclosed to transform them into state monopolies for commercial exploitation. In the rural areas, effects on the peasants were gradual erosion of usufruct rights of access to food, fuel and livestock grazing from the community's common lands. The marginalization of the rights of peasant communities over their forests, sacred groves and wastelands has been the prime cause of their impoverishment.

Biodiversity has always been a local community-owned and utilized resource for indigenous communities. A resource is common property when social systems exist to use it on the principles of justice and sustainability. This involves a combination of rights and responsibilities among users, a combination of utilization and conservation, a sense of co-production with nature and sharing among members of diverse communities. They do not view their heritage in terms of property at all, i.e., a good which has an owner and is used for the purpose of extracting economic benefits, but instead they view it in terms of possessing community and individual responsibility. For indigenous people, heritage is a bundle of relationships rather than a bundle of economic rights. That is the reason no concept of 'private property' existed among the communities for common resources.

Within indigenous communities, despite some innovations

being first introduced by individuals, innovation is seen as a social and collective phenomenon and results of innovation are freely available to anyone who wants to use them. Consequently, not only the biodiversity but its utilization has also been in the commons, being freely exchanged both within and between communities. Common resource knowledge based innovations have been passed on over centuries to new generations and adopted for newer uses, and these innovations have over time been absorbed into the common pool of knowledge about that resource. This common pool of knowledge has contributed immeasurably to the vast agricultural and medicinal plant diversity that exists today. Thus, the concept of individual 'property' rights to either the resource or to knowledge remain alien to the local community. This undoubtedly exacerbates the usurpation of the knowledge of indigenous people with serious consequences for them and for biodiversity conservation.

Commons and communities are governed by self-determined norms and are self-managed. In the 'colonial' and 'development' era, the commons were enclosed and community power undermined by the state. Water and forests were made state property, leading to the alienation of local communities and destruction of the resource base. Poverty, ecological destruction, social disintegration and political disempowerment have been the result of such state-driven 'enclosures'.

Today we have to look beyond the state and the market place to protect the rights of the majority of Indians—the rural communities. Empowering the community with rights would enable the recovery of the commons. Commons are resources shaped, managed and utilized through community control. In the commons, no one can be excluded. The commons cannot be monopolized by the economically powerful citizen or corporations or by the politically powerful state. While tribals and rural communities are still overwhelmed by state-driven 'enclosures', tools for new corporate and WTO-driven 'enclosures' are being shaped in the form of patents on life and biodiversity.

The biological diversity of India has always been a common resource for millions of our traditional communities, who have utilized, protected and conserved their biodiversity heritage over centuries. Their collective and cumulative innovation has been the basis of local culture and local economies, which constitute the dominant economies in terms of the livelihoods provided and the needs met. In fact, traditional knowledge in medicine, agriculture and fisheries is the primary base for meeting food and health needs. For many communities, conserving biodiversity means conserving the integrity of the ecosystem and species, the right to resources and knowledge and the right to the production systems based on this biodiversity. Therefore, biodiversity is intimately linked to traditional indigenous knowledge systems as well as to people's rights to protect their knowledge and resources.

Biopiracy

What is Biopiracy?

BIOPIRACY REFERS TO THE use of intellectual property systems to legitimize the exclusive ownership and control over biological resources and biological products and processes that have been used over centuries in non-industrialized cultures. Patent claims over biodiversity and indigenous knowledge that are based on the innovation, creativity and genius of the people of the Third World are acts of 'biopiracy'. Since a 'patent' is given for invention, a biopiracy patent denies the innovation embodied in indigenous knowledge. The rush to grant patents and reward invention has led corporations and governments in the industrialized world to ignore the centuries of cumulative, collective innovation of generations of rural communities.

Biopiracy occurs because of the inadequacy of western patent systems and the inherent western bias against other cultures. Western patent systems were designed for import monopolies, not for screening all knowledge systems to exclude existing innovations and establish *prior art* in other cultures. Western culture has also suffered from the 'Columban blunder' of the right to plunder by treating other people, their rights, and their knowledge as non-existent. *Terra nullius* has its contemporary equivalent in 'Bio-Nullius'— treating biodiversity knowledge as empty of prior creativity and prior rights, and hence available for 'ownership' through the claim to 'invention'.

When applied to knowledge related to biodiversity, reductionism isolates chemicals and genes and treats this act of separation as an act of creation, both intellectually and materially. The leads for useful traits in biological organisms are obtained from indigenous knowledge. Ninety-four per cent of the top-selling plant-derived drugs contain at least one compound that has a demonstrated use in traditional medicine related to primary therapeutic use. The appropriation of indigenous knowledge and of the uses of biodiversity is not a creative act at either the intellectual or at the material level. Intellectually, the innovation has already been done as part of indigenous knowledge systems. Materially, the traits and properties for which the patent has been claimed already exist in nature. Their isolation and separation cannot be claimed as creation. Treating translation and transfer of existing indigenous knowledge and isolation of useful traits of life forms as acts of 'creation' and 'invention' is rooted in the philosophical assumptions of the industrial society which defines non-western cultures as inferior to the industrial west and perceives nature as inert, dead matter. The creativity of both nature and other cultures is negated, and appropriation of that creativity is then interpreted as an act of creation.

With knowledge plurality mutating into knowledge hierarchy, a horizontal ordering of diverse but equally valid and diverse systems is converted into a vertical ordering of unequal systems, with the epistemological foundations of the system being imposed on others to invalidate them. This translation of knowledge diversities into knowledge hierarchies is then used to claim acts of translation as acts of invention. Translation is misconstrued as the 'creation' of knowledge. A sociological shift is thus fallaciously treated as an epistemological shift. This fallacy of sociological and cultural displacement as an epistemological shift generating new knowledge is made possible as a result of colonial biases which have treated western knowledge as exclusively scientific and non-western knowledge systems as unscientific. However, the difference in epistemological foundations does not make indigenous knowledge systems inferior; it just makes them different.

This diversity of knowledge needs to be recognized and respected, and a pluralistic IPR regime needs to be evolved which makes it possible to recognize and respect indigenous knowledge, and protect the indigenous knowledge systems and practices and livelihoods based on it. We, therefore, need diverse legal regimes to protect the diverse knowledge systems and the diverse communities. The legal regime being universalized through TRIPs and WTO is restricted to western IPR systems reflecting the interest of the dominant economic systems of the west—the MNCs.

When an element from indigenous knowledge systems is transferred to western knowledge systems, it is treated as an innovation in western systems. As a corollary, the interests and rights of non-western communities find no place in western legal systems and are instead transferred to the scientific practitioners of western knowledge systems, in particular, those backed by corporate capital. Western systems of knowledge in agriculture and medicine were defined as the only scientific system. Indigenous systems of knowledge were defined as inferior, and in fact, unscientific. Thus, instead of strengthening research on safe and sustainable plant-based pesticides such as *neem* and *pongamia*, we focused exclusively on the development and promotion of hazardous and non-sustainable chemical pesticides such as DDT and Sevin. Unfortunately, the use of DDT has increased the occurrence of pests 12,000-fold. The manufacture of Sevin at the Union Carbide Plant in Bhopal led to the Bhopal gas leak disaster which killed thousands and has disabled more than 400,000 people.

Meanwhile, as a recognition of the ecological failure of the chemical route to pest control, the use of plant-based pesticides is becoming popular in the industrialized world. Corporations that have promoted the use of chemicals are now looking for biological options. In the search for new markets and control over the biodiversity base for the production of biopesticides and chemicals, MNCs are claiming IPRs on *neem*-based biopesticides.

This experience with agrichemicals is also replicated in the field of drugs and medicines as well. Ironically, as a result of increasing public awareness of the side effects of hazardous drugs and the rise of strains resistant to antibiotics, the western pharmaceutical industry is increasingly turning to the plant-based system of Indian and Chinese medicine. Indigenous medical systems are based on over 7,000 species of medicinal plants and on 15,000 medicines of herbal formulations in different systems. The Ayurvedic texts refer to 1,400 plants, Unani texts to 342, the Siddha system to 328. Homeopathy uses 570, of which approximately 100 are Indian plants. The economic value of medicinal plants to 100 million rural households is unmeasurable.

Patenting of drugs derived from indigenous systems of medicine has started to take on epidemic proportions. The current value of the world market for medicinal plants from leads given by indigenous and local communities is estimated to be $43 billion. Using traditional knowledge has increased the efficiency of screening plants for medical properties by more than 40 per cent.

This phenomena of 'biopiracy' in which western commercial interests claim products and innovations derived from and currently used by indigenous knowledge traditions as their 'intellectual property' protected through 'intellectual property rights' like patents has emerged as a result of the devaluation, and hence the invisibility, of indigenous systems. This devaluation is linked to the imposition of the reductionist methods of western science to the non-reductionist approaches of indigenous knowledge systems. Further, since western-style IPR systems are biased towards western knowledge systems which reduce biodiversity to its chemical or genetic structures, the indigenous systems get no protection, but piracy of these systems is protected.

While the IPR debate during the Uruguay Round of GATT negotiations was framed on the grounds that stricter, western-style IPR regimes were needed globally to prevent piracy by the South, in recent years it has become evident that piracy is in fact being undertaken by corporations of the North which are appropriating the biodiversity and indigenous knowledge of the South. In the absence of a protection system for biodiversity and indigenous knowledge systems, and with the universalization of western-style IPR regimes, such intellectual and biological piracy will grow. Protecting our biological and intellectual heritage in the age of biopiracy requires the recognition and rejunevation of our heritage, and the evolution of legal systems for the protection of this heritage in the context of emerging IPR regimes.

Stealing from the Pharmacy of the Poor

Indian systems of medicine—Ayurveda, Unani and Siddha—and folk traditions have used various plants for the treatment of common diseases. *Phyllanthus niruri* is one such medicinal plant used widely all over India for the treatment of various forms of hepatitis and other liver disorders. It is as much a part of formal health care systems as it is part of local health practices, folk medicine and traditional indigenous collective knowledge. The plant is called *Bhudharti* in Sanskrit, *Jar amla* in Hindi and *Bhuin amla* in Bengali.

It is common throughout the hotter parts of India, growing in fallow land and in shade. An annual herb, 10-30 cm. high, its leaves are elliptic-oblong like the *amla* (hence the name *Jar amla* or *Bhuin amla*). It flowers and fruits from April to September. The entire plant—its leaves, shoots and roots— is used for treating jaundice. Even though the use of *Phyllanthus niruri* for the treatment of jaundice has been an ancient and well recorded innovation in the Indian systems of medicine, patents are now being applied for this knowledge as if it were a novel invention.

The Fox Chase Cancer Centre of Philadelphia, USA, has applied to the European Patent Office for the use of *Phyllanthus niruri* in curing hepatitis. The patent claim is for the manufacture of a medicament for the treatment of viral hepatitis B. The patent application refers to Dr. K.M. Nadkarni's *Indian Materia Medica* which reports that formulations based on *Phyllanthus niruri* are used for treatment of jaundice in classical and folk traditions. In spite of the prior knowledge of its use as a cure for all forms of hepatitis, including hepatitis B, the Fox Chase cancer claim states that *Phyllanthus niruri* has not been proposed for the treatment of viral hepatitis infection prior to the work done by the inventors of the present invention.

In allopathic systems there is no specific treatment for jaundice. In case of viral hepatitis, an attempt is made to provide symptomatic treatment by giving glucose, Vitamin B complex, and avoiding fatty and fried foods. In Ayurveda and other traditional systems of medicine, there are products which are known to help in the regeneration of the liver tissue. This treatment is therefore addressed to the root cause of the health problem and not just its symptoms. Since in traditional systems of medicine the diagnosis of jaundice is made on the basis of it being a problem associated with liver function, it is immaterial what strain of infective hepatitis it is, since the management of all infective hepatitis is essentially the same.

By isolating the application of *Phyllanthus niruri* for the treatment of one form of infective hepatitis only, i.e., hepatitis B, and treating this as a novel application, even though medicines derived from *Phyllanthus niruri* have been used for treating all forms of hepatitis in traditional systems of medicine, scientists of the Fox Chase Cancer Centre have falsely presented an act of piracy as an act of invention.

The latest patents on the anti-diabetic properties of *karela*, *jamun*, and *brinjal* once again highlight the problem of biopiracy. The use of *karela*, *jamun* and *brinjal* for control of diabetes is everyday knowledge and practised in India. Their use in the treatment of diabetes is documented in authoritative treatises like the *Wealth of India*, the *Compendium of Indian Medicinal Plants* and the *Treatise on Indian Medicinal Plants*. The claim to the use of *karela* or *jamun* for anti-diabetic treatment as an invention is false since such use has been known and documented widely in India. The US patent granted recently to Cromak Research Inc. based in New Jersey for the use of these plants in the cure of diabetes is a clear case of intellectual piracy coupled with the arrogance in assuming that these resources become 'value added' when processed in western laboratories. Such a patent also has a serious negative impact on the possible export market for formulations by Indian drug companies that meet the requirement of Indian systems of medicine.

Stealing from the Farms of our Farmers

The Indian subcontinent is the biggest producer and exporter of superfine aromatic rice—basmati. India grows 650,000 tonnes of basmati annually. Basmati covers 10–15 per cent of the total land area under rice cultivation in India. Non-basmati and basmati rice is exported to more than eighty countries across the world. Non-basmati rice exports in 1996–97 were 1.9 million tonnes and amounted to Rs 18 billion ($450 million), while basmati exports were 488,700 tonnes and fetched the exchequer Rs 11.2 billion ($280 million). Annual basmati exports are between 400,000 to 500,000 tonnes. Basmati rice has been one of the fastest growing export items from India in recent years. The main importers of Indian basmati are the Middle East (65 per cent), Europe (20 per cent) and USA (10–15 per cent). At $850 a tonne, Indian basmati is the most expensive rice being imported by the European Union (EU) compared to $700 a tonne for Pakistani basmati and $500 a tonne for Thai fragrant rice. Indian basmati exports to the EU in 1996–97 amounted to nearly 100,000 tonnes.

Basmati has been grown for centuries in the subcontinent as is evident from references in ancient texts, folklore and poetry. There are twenty-seven distinct documented varieties of basmati grown in India. One of the earliest references to basmati according to the CSS Haryana Agricultural University, Hissar, is made in the famous epic of *Heer Ranjha*, written by the poet Varis Shah in 1766. This naturally-perfumed variety of rice has always been treasured and possessively guarded by nobles since time immemorial, and eagerly coveted by foreigners. It has evolved over centuries of observation, experimentation and selection by farmers who have developed numerous varieties of the rice to meet various ecological conditions, cooking needs and tastes. Informal breeding and innovation have resulted in the superior qualities of this rice and must therefore predominantly be recognized as the contribution of the subcontinent's farmers.

On 2 September 1997, Texas-based RiceTec Inc. was granted patent number 5663484 on basmati rice lines and grains. The patent of this 'invention' is exceptionally broad and includes twenty claims within it. The patent covers the genetic lines of the basmati and includes genes from the varieties developed by farmers. It thus automatically covers farmers' varieties and if enforced, farmers will not be able to grow these varieties developed by them and their forefathers without getting permission for and paying royalty to RiceTec. RiceTec has already been trading under brand names such as Kasmati, Texmati and Jasmati.

RiceTec's strain possesses the same qualities—long grain, distinct aroma, high-yielding and semi-dwarf in stature—as our Indian traditional varieties. As the RiceTec line is essentially derived from basmati, it cannot be claimed as 'novel' and therefore should not be patentable.

Stealing Nature's Pesticide

Neem, or *Azadirachta indica*, has been used for diverse purposes over centuries in India. It has been used in medicine and in agriculture. The *neem* is mentioned in Indian texts written over 2000 years ago as an air purifier and as a cure for almost all types of human and animal diseases because of its insect- and pest-repellant properties. It is used on every farm, in every house, almost everyday in India. Research has shown that *neem* extracts can influence nearly 200 species of insects, many of which are resistant to pesticides. A number of *neem*-based commercial products, including pesticides, medicines and cosmetics, have come on the Indian market in recent years, some of them produced in the small-scale sector, others by medium-sized laboratories. However, there has been no attempt to acquire proprietary ownership of formulae, since, under the 1970 Patent Act of India, agricultural and medicinal products are not patentable.

The combination of the *neem*'s cultural, medicinal and agricultural values have contributed to its widespread distribution and propagation. More than 50,000 *neem* trees shelter pilgrims on the way to Mecca. Indians have gifted knowledge about the *neem* to the entire world. The existence of diverse species and the freedom with which knowledge can be exchanged is best symbolized by the *neem*.

The *neem* is therefore referred to as the 'free tree' of India. For centuries the western world ignored the *neem* tree and its properties; the practices of Indian peasants and doctors were not deemed worthy of attention by the majority of British, French and Portuguese colonialists. However, in the last few years, growing opposition to chemical products in the west, in particular to pesticides, has led to a sudden enthusiasm for the pharmaceutical properties of *neem*. In 1971, US timber importer Robert Larson observed the tree's usefulness in India and began importing *neem* seed to his company headquarters in Wisconsin. Over the next decade, he conducted safety and performance tests upon a pesticidal *neem* extract called Margosan-O and in 1985 received clearance for the product from the US Environmental Protection Agency (EPA). Three years later, he sold the patent for the product to the multinational chemical corporation, W.R. Grace. Since 1985, over a dozen US patents have been taken out by US and Japanese firms on formulae for stable *neem*-based solutions and emulsions and even for a *neem*-based toothpaste.

Having garnered their patents and with the prospect of a licence from EPA, Grace has set about manufacturing and commercializing their product by establishing a base in India. The company approached several Indian manufacturers with proposals to buy up their technology or to convince them to stop producing value-added products and instead supply the company with raw material. In many cases, W.R. Grace met with a rebuff. Eventually, it managed to arrange a joint venture with a firm called PJ Margo Pvt. Ltd. They have set up a plant in India which processes upto 20 tonnes of seed a day. They are also setting up a network of *neem* seed suppliers to ensure a constant supply of the seeds at a reliable price. Grace is likely to be followed by other patent-holding companies.

The company's demand for seed had had three primary effects:

1. The price of *neem* seed has risen beyond the reach of the ordinary people; in fact, *neem* oil itself, used by local people to light lamps, is practically unavailable any more as local oil millers are not able to access the seed.
2. Almost all the seed collected, which was freely available to the farmer and the indigenous health practitioner, is purchased by the company because of its economic power.
3. Poor people have lost access to a resource vital for their survival—a resource that was once widely and cheaply available to them.

In 1992, the US National Research Council published a report designed to 'open up the western world's corporate eyes to the seemingly endless variety of products the tree might offer.' According to one of the members of the NRC panel, 'In this day and age, when we're not very happy about synthetic pesticides, *neem* has great appeal.' This appeal is blatantly commercial. The US pesticides market is worth about $2 billion. At the moment, biopesticides constitute about $450 million of this, but the figure was close to $800 million by 1998.

The *neem* tree itself has not been patented, nor have its parts such as leaves, twigs, roots, stems, etc. However, certain processes and products which involve various active principles of the *neem* have been patented. Grace's aggressive interest in Indian *neem* production has provoked a chorus of objections from Indian scientists, farmers and political activists, who assert that multinational companies have no right to expropriate the fruit of centuries of indigenous experimentation and several decades of Indian scientific research. This has stimulated a bitter transcontinental debate about the ethics of intellectual property and patent rights. W.R. Grace's justification for patents pivots on the claim that these modernized extraction processes constitute a genuine innovation. Although traditional knowledge inspired the research and development that led to these patented compositions and processes, they were considered sufficiently novel and different from the original product of nature and the traditional method of use to be patentable.

In short, the processes are supposedly novel and an advance on Indian techniques. However, this novelty exists mainly in the context of the ignorance of the west. Over the 2,000 years that *neem*-based biopesticides and medicines have been used in India, many complex processes have been developed to make them available for specific use, though the active ingredients were not given Latinized 'scientific' names. Common knowledge and common use of *neem* was one of the primary reasons given by the Indian Central Insecticide Board for not registering *neem* products under the Insecticides Act, 1968. The Board argued that *neem* materials had been in extensive use in India for various purposes since time immemorial, without any known deleterious effects. The US EPA, on the other hand, does not accept the validity of traditional knowledge.

The reluctance of Indian scientists to patent their inventions, thus leaving their work vulnerable to piracy, may in part derive from a recognition that the bulk of the work had already been accomplished by generations of anonymous experimenters. The discovery of *neem*'s pesticidal properties and of how to process it was by no means 'obvious', but evolved through extended systematic knowledge development in non-western cultures.

The *neem* is thus no longer a 'free tree' and has more than ninety patents on it today including patent claims by American, Japanese and German companies. It is now the 'intellectual property' of western scientists and corporations. However, more than 200 organizations have legally challenged two of the *neem* patents held by W.R. Grace, one in the US and one in the European Patent Office. On 10 May 2000, a major milestone was crossed in the contemporary movement for freedom from biopiracy when the European Patent Office struck down the patent jointly owned by the US government and W.R. Grace as based on the piracy of existing knowledge and lacking in novelty and inventiveness.

Resolving Biopiracy

Biopiracy and patenting of indigenous knowledge is a double theft because first it allows theft of creativity and innovation, and secondly, the exclusive rights established by patents on stolen knowledge steal economic options of everyday survival on the basis of indigenous biodiversity and knowledge. Over time, the patents can be used to create monopolies and make everyday products highly priced. If there were only one or two cases of such false claims to invention on the basis of biopiracy, they could be called an error. However, biopiracy is an epidemic. The problem is not, as was made out to be in the case of turmeric, an error made by a patent clerk. The problem is deep and systemic. And it calls for a systemic change, not a case-by-case challenge.

The promotion of piracy is not an aberration in the US patent law. It is intrinsic to it. IPR regimes in the context of free trade and trade liberalization become instruments of piracy at three levels:

1. *Resource piracy* in which the biological and natural resources of communities and the country are freely taken, without recognition or permission, and are used to build up global economies. For example, the transfer of basmati varieties of rice from India to build the rice economy of US corporations like RiceTec for export.

2. *Intellectual and cultural piracy* in which the cultural and intellectual heritage of communities and the country is freely taken without recognition or permission and is used for claiming IPRs such as patents and trademark even though the primary innovation and creativity, has not taken place through corporate investment. For instance, the use of the trade name 'basmati' for their aromatic rice, or Pepsi's use of the trade name *Bikaneri bhujia*.

3. *Economic piracy* in which the domestic and international markets are usurped through the use of trade names and IPRs, thereby destroying local economies and national economies where the original innovation took place and hence wiping out the livelihoods and economic survival of millions. For example, US rice traders usurping European markets and Grace usurping the US market from small-scale Indian producers of *neem*-based biopesticides.

The problem of biopiracy is a result of western-style IPR

systems, not the absence of such IPR systems in India. An argument is often made that the western patent system works and that biopiracy can be corrected by a case-by-case challenge. This is false for two reasons. Firstly, patent challenges are costly, and Third World countries cannot keep up with the expenditure of challenging the hundreds of biopiracy cases that are growing. Secondly, the case of the revocation of the turmeric patent on the basis of a challenge by CSIR in 1996 has not stopped the US Patent and Trade Mark Office (USPTO) from granting fresh patents for turmeric. The USPTO granted a patent on 27 April 1999 for the use of turmeric for skin disorders.

Individual challenges will not stop biopiracy. The IPR system itself has to undergo change. If a patent system which is supposed to reward inventiveness and creativity systematically rewards piracy, if a patent system fails to honestly apply criteria of novelty and non-obviousness in the granting of patents related to indigenous knowledge, then the system is flawed and it needs to change. It cannot be the basis of granting patents or establishing exclusive marketing rights.

BIOPROSPECTING AS LEGALIZED BIOPIRACY

A common proposal offered as a solution to biopiracy is that of bioprospecting and benefit sharing, i.e., those who claim patents on indigenous knowledge should share benefits from the profits of their commercial monopolies with the original innovators. Bioprospecting is being promoted as the model for relationships between corporations who commercialize indigenous knowledge and indigenous communities which have collectively innovated and evolved the knowledge.

However, bioprospecting is merely a sophisticated form of biopiracy. There are two basic problems with this model. Firstly, if knowledge already exists, a patent based on it is totally un-justified since it violates the principles of novelty and non-obviousness. Granting patents for indigenous knowledge amounts to stating that the patent system is about power and control, not inventiveness and novelty. Secondly, the appropriation of indigenous knowledge vital for food and medicine, its conversion into an exclusive right through patents, and the establishment of an economic system in which people have to buy what they had produced for themselves is a system which denies benefits and creates impoverishment, not a process which promotes 'benefit sharing'. It is the equivalent of stealing a loaf of bread and then sharing the crumbs.

Bioprospecting, in effect, leads to the enclosure of the biological and intellectual commons. It takes the biodiversity and intellectual heritage of indigenous communities and converts it into commodities protected by IPRs. Collective innovation evolving over time and involving many persons is different from individual innovation localized in time and space. Collective innovation involves many persons who contribute to it over time. It is modified and enhanced as it is used over time and passed on from generation to generation. In some examples such collective innovation is no longer local, e.g., in the case of seeds and in the case of major non-western knowledge traditions such as Ayurvedic and Chinese medicine. In some cases it even crosses national boundaries.

In the context of privatization, the mutual exchange among communities has been replaced by contracts for bioprospecting by corporations who seek to expropriate invaluable and inalienable heritage of communities, often through scientific collection missions and ethno-botanic research. The World Resources Institute has defined 'biodiversity prospecting' as exploration of commercially valuable genetic and biochemical resources. The metaphor for prospecting is borrowed from the prospecting for 'gold' or 'oil'. While biodiversity is fast becoming the 'green gold' and 'green oil' for the pharmaceutical and biotechnology industry, the metaphor for prospecting suggests that prior to prospecting, the resource lies buried, unknown, unused and without value. However, unlike gold or oil deposits, the uses and value of biodiversity are known to local communities, from where the knowledge is taken through bioprospecting contracts. The metaphor of bioprospecting thus hides the prior uses and knowledge and rights associated with it. Taking knowledge from indigenous communities through bioprospecting is only the first step in developing an IPR protected industrial system which must eventually market commodities that have used local knowledge as an input, but are not based on the ethical, epistemological, or ecological structures of that knowledge system. They use biodiversity fragments as 'raw material' to produce biological products protected by patents that displace the biodiversity and indigenous knowledge which they have exploited. Bioprospecting is the first step towards occupying the dominant system of monocultures and monopolies and thus accepting the destruction of diversity.

Indigenous knowledge is centred on co-creation by nature and people. IPR regimes are premised on the denial of the creativity of nature. The ethical and epistemological assumptions and consequences of adopting an IPR regime through bioprospecting contracts needs deeper analysis and reflection. The bioprospecting paradigm needs to be examined in the context of equity, specifically its impacts on the donor community, the recipient communities and on bioprospecting corporations.

Even though bioprospecting contracts are based on prior informed consent and compensation, unlike biopiracy where no consent is taken and no compensation given, not all owners/ carriers of an indigenous knowledge tradition are consulted or compensated. Not only does this lead to inequity and injustice, it also has the potential of putting individual against individual within a community and community against community in a community of communities. This is the reason bioprospecting models which deal with one individual or one community or one interest group can never be equitable. A commercial interest needs to take the prior informed consent of *all* communities and *all* members of each community who have used and contributed to collective innovation in biodiversity-related knowledge. The partnership of the state is one mechanism for the interests of all contributing groups. In the case of biodiversity-related collective innovation there are many interests involved. Farmers and the seed industry, traditional healers and pharmaceutical corporations, western and non-western scientific traditions, masculinist ways of knowing and feminist ways of knowing. All the diverse communities of interest have to be included in a transaction.

Collective rights cannot be abjured or relinquished by any one community of users, or any individual of any community, or the state on behalf of any community. The bioprospecting model, therefore, is not a legitimate source of benefit sharing in the case of biodiversity-related knowledge. It is based on a double exclusion. The first exclusion takes place when communities of users/innovators are excluded and one local group is treated as holding the knowledge exclusively. The second exclusion takes place when the commercial enterprise signing a bioprospecting contract takes an IPR on the knowledge transferred from an indigenous community as an unjustified claim to innovation. Over time, this excludes the donor community itself, as marketing systems and IPR regimes combine to make the community providing biological resources and knowledge dependent on the purchase of proprietary commodities from the corporations who monopolize the biodiversity and knowledge, e.g., farmers who contributed seed having to buy proprietary seed from the seed industry.

Bioprospecting is often presented as a means for making the poor rich. It is often stated that regions rich in biodiversity are financially poor and since bioprospecting is associated with monetary compensation, it can make such regions financially rich also. However, the bioprospecting model is a model for taking away the last resources, both natural and intellectual, from the poor. It is, therefore, in reality, a model for creating poverty for the community as a whole even when it might bring money to a few individuals in the community.

The poverty-creating impact of biopiracy and bioprospecting can only be perceived if one recognizes that there is a difference between the material economy and the financial economy. If people have rich biodiversity and intellectual wealth, they can meet their needs for health care and nutrition through their own resources and their knowledge. If, on the other hand, the rights to both resources and knowledge have been transferred from the community to IPR holders, the members of a community end up paying high prices or royalties for what was originally theirs and which they had for free. They, therefore, become materially poorer.

When biodiversity knowledge of a community is taken by a corporation which commercializes it and transforms it into proprietary knowledge protected by IPRs, a number of impacts are felt by the donor community.

1. Free receiving but proprietary sales and prohibition of free exchange between individuals and communities leads to monopoly control over biodiversity and knowledge.

2. As biodiversity gains commercial value globally, e.g., a medicinal plant, it is exploited. This leads to diversion of the biological resource from meeting local needs to feeding non-local greed. This generates scarcity, thus leading to price increases.

3. In the case of over-exploitation it can lead to extinction.

4. The local scarcity combined with IPRs on derived commodities eventually takes the resource and its products beyond the access of the donor communities (e.g., *neem*).

5. The providing communities lose their rightful share to emerging markets.

6. Other poor communities (whose traditions permit them to rely on free exchange or low cost seed) which could have received the knowledge freely or at low cost are also made dependent on the commercial interest.

This perspective reflects the bioprospecting or commodity paradigm which only protects the rights of those who appropriate people's common resources and turns them into commodities. As discussed, the benefits provided and shared by indigenous and local communities are rendered invisible and the focus is only on the benefits shared by those who privatize and enclose the commons. In my opinion, reclaiming the intellectual commons through asserting collective intellectual property rights represents the real model of equitable benefit sharing. Equitable benefit sharing in the domain of indigenous knowledge and biodiversity is inconsistent with the monopolies and exclusive rights which patents guarantee. Outlawing biopiracy and making patents based on the piracy of indigenous knowledge illegal is thus necessary for guaranteeing equity and sustainability.

Can Seed be Owned?

Seed: The Ultimate Gift

SEED IS THE FIRST link in the food chain. It is the embodiment of life's continuity and renewability; of life's biological and cultural diversity. Seed, for the farmer, is not merely a source of future plants/food; it is the storage place of culture, of history. Seed is the ultimate symbol of food security.

Free exchange of seed among farmers has been the basis of maintaining biodiversity as well as food security. This exchange is based on cooperation and reciprocity. A farmer who wants to exchange seed generally gives an equal quantity of seed from his field in return for the seed he gets.

Free exchange among farmers goes beyond mere exchange of seeds; it also involves exchange of ideas and knowledge, of culture and heritage. It is an accumulation of tradition, of knowledge of how to work the seed. Farmers gather knowledge about the seeds they want to grow in the future by watching them actually grow in other farmers' fields. The cultural and religious significance of the plant, gastronomic, drought and disease resistance, pest resistance, keeping, and other values shape the knowledge that the community accords to the seed and the plant it produces.

Paddy, for example, has religious significance in most parts of India and is an essential component of most religious festivals.

The *Akti* festival in Chhattisgarh, a centre of diversity of the *Indica* variety of rice, reinforces the many principles of biodiversity conservation. In the South, rice grain is mixed with *kumkum* (vermilion) and turmeric and given as a blessing. The priest is given rice, often along with a coconut, as an indication of religious regard. Other agricultural produce whose seeds, leaves, or flower form an essential component of religious ceremonies include coconut, betel leaves, arecanut, wheat, finger and little millets, horse gram, black gram, chickpea, pigeon pea, sesame, sugarcane, jack fruit seed, cardamom, ginger, banana and gooseberry.

New seeds are first worshipped and then planted. The new crop is worshipped before being consumed. Both these festivals—planting and harvest—are celebrated in the fields and symbolize people's intimacy with nature. At the time of planting, the field is seen as mother; worshipping the field is a sign of gratitude towards the earth, who as mother feeds the millions of life forms who are her children. Festivals like *Ugadi, Ramanavami, Akshay Trateeya, Ekadashi Aluyana Amavase, Naga Panchami, Noolu Hunime, Ganesh Chaturthi, Rishi Panchami, Navratri, Deepavali, Rathasaptami, Tulsi Vivaha Campasrusti* and *Bhoomi Puja* cannot be celebrated without religious ceremonies around the seed. Seed festivals include those related to identification of which seed to grow, its germination and other aspects.

According to Hindu mythology, seed is a gift of Srushtikarta (Brahma, the creator), who created seeds in primordial times. The *Puranas* refer to people getting *fala* (fruit/reward) by worshipping gods through religious sacrifices. In the case of complete extinction of any one form of matter, the people performed *samudra manthana* (churning the ocean) to get it back. Indian agricultural folklore includes instances of kings who ploughed the land to plant seed. Janaka, the father of Sita, worshipped Varuna (god of rain) during a drought and got a handful of seed from him, which he planted after ploughing the land himself, so that his people would not go hungry. Seed is also considered and worshipped as Dhanalakshmi (the goddess of wealth).

In Indian culture, all forms of nature are believed to interact with and influence one another, be they of this earth or of space. This interaction and influence is often reflected in the linking of cosmic influences of planets and stars to life forms on earth. The *navadhanyas* (nine seeds) and their respect *navagrahas* (nine cosmic influences) symbolize balance in the field and a reflexive relationship in the Ayurveda tradition. The relationship of some of the seeds and the *graha* is given below:

Seeds and their Cosmic Influences

Seed	Graha (Cosmic Influence)	Dhatu (Representing Body Element)	Disease/Symptom
Barley (*Yava*)	Sun (*Ravi*)	Bone (*Ashthii*)	Excessive digestive power, pain, fever
Little Millet (*Shamaka*)	Moon (*Chandra*)	Blood (*Rakhta*), Muscular Tissue (*Maamsa*)	Vomiting, constipation, diarrhoea, thirst, giddiness
Pigeon Pea (*Togari*)	Mars (*Mangala*)	Bone marrow (*Majja*)	Bleeding, ulcers
Mung (*Magda*)	Mercury (*Budha*)	Skin (*Twach*)	Pain, fever, mental disorder
Chick Pea (*Kadale*)	Jupiter (*Brihaspati*)	Adipose (*Vasa*)	Mental illness
Sesame (*Til*)	Saturn (*Shani*)	Minute vessels (*Arotha*)	Thirst, tastelessness

Seed not only plays a important part in the rituals and rites of communities, it also represents the accumulation over centuries of people's knowledge and, by being a reflection of the options available to them, it represents their choice. In today's context of biological and ecological destruction, seed conservors are the true gifters of seed. Conserving seed is thus more than merely conserving germplasm. Conserving seed is conserving biodiversity, conserving knowledge of the seed and its utilization, conserving culture, conserving sustainability.

The culture of seed saving and seed exchange which has been the basis of Indian agriculture is today under threat. New technologies, like the technologies of the green revolution and biotechnologies, devalue the cultural and traditional knowledge embodied in the seed and erode the holistic knowledge of the seed from the community. This results in the seed itself becoming extinct, as the existence of the seed is tied intimately with its holistic knowledge.

This process is being hastened by the new IPR regimes which are being universalized through TRIPs. The IPR regimes of the west allow corporations to usurp the knowledge of the seed and monopolize it by claiming it to be their private property. Over time, this results in monopolistic corporate control over the seed itself, restricting its free sharing within and across communities.

New intellectual property rights are being introduced through the WTO in the form of patents or breeders' rights. Patents on plants and seeds imply that corporations which have the patent can claim that a seed or plant or crop variety is their invention and exclude others from making, selling, using, or distributing the seed or crop. The ancient system of saving seed or exchanging seeds freely with neighbours is thus viewed as 'intellectual property theft' under IPR regimes. Companies are already taking farmers to court in industrialized countries for seed saving and seed exchange.

There are two ways in which farmers' rights and freedoms related to agricultural systems and seeds are being eroded. Firstly, seed legislation pushes out farmers' varieties and makes farmers' breeding an illegal activity. Secondly, farmers are forced to give up their inalienable rights to save, exchange and improve seed. This forces farmers to use only 'registered' varieties. Since farmers' varieties are not registered and individual small farmers cannot afford the costs of registration, they are slowly pushed into dependence on corporations who sell 'registered' seed varieties.

Seed Legislation

There are many examples of how Seed Acts in various countries and the introduction of IPRs prevent farmers from engaging in their own seed production. Josef Albrecht, an organic farmer in Germany, was not satisfied with the commercially available seed. He worked and developed his own ecological varieties of wheat. Ten other organic farmers from neighbouring villages took his wheat seeds. Albrecht was fined by his government because he traded in uncertified seed. He has challenged the penalty and the Seed Act because he feels restricted in freely exercising his occupation as an organic farmer by this law.

In Scotland, there are a large number of farmers who grow seed potato and sell seed potato to other farmers. They could, until the early 1990s, freely sell the reproductive material to other seed potato growers, to merchants, or to farmers. In the 1990s, holders of plant breeders' rights started to issue notices to potato growers through the British Society of Plant Breeders and made selling of seed potato by farmers to other farmers illegal. Seed potato growers had to grow varieties under contract to the seed industry, which specified the price at which the contracting company would take back the crop and barred growers from selling the crop to anyone. Soon, the companies started to reduce the acreage and prices. In 1994, seed potato bought from Scottish farmers for £140 was sold for more than double that price to English farmers, whilst the two sets of farmers were prevented from dealing directly with each other. Seed potato growers signed a petition complaining about the stranglehold of a few companies acting as a 'cartel'. They also started to sell non-certified seed directly to English farmers. The seed industry claimed they were losing £4 million in seed sales through the direct sale of uncertified seed potato between farmers. In February 1995, the British Society for Plant Breeders decided to proceed with a high profile court case against a farmer from Aberdeenshire. The farmer was forced to pay £30,000 as compensation to cover royalties lost to the seed industry by direct farmer-to-farmer exchange. Existing United Kingdom and European Union laws thus prevent farmers from exchanging uncertified seed as well as protected varieties.

In the US as well, farmer-to-farmer exchange has been made illegal. Dennis and Becky Winterboer were farmers owning a 500-acre farm in Iowa. Since 1987, the Winterboers have derived a sizeable portion of their income from 'brown bagging' sales of their crops to other farmers to use as seed. A 'brown bag' sale occurs when a farmer plants seeds in his own field and then sells the harvest as seed to other farmers. Asgrow (a commercial company which has plant variety protection for its soybean seeds) filed suit against the Winterboers on the grounds that its property rights were being violated. The Winterboers argued that they had acted within the law since according to the Plant Variety Act farmers had the right to sell seed, provided both the farmer and seller were farmers.

Subsequently, in 1994, the Plant Variety Act was amended, and the farmers' privilege to save and exchange seed was amended, establishing absolute monopoly of the seed industry by making farmer-to-farmer exchange and sales illegal.

Then there is the case of Monsanto's Round-Up-Ready Gene Agreement. Under this agreement, Monsanto, a major seed company, prevents farmers from selling or supplying the seed or material derived from their crop to any other person or entity, or saving any of the seed. The agreement also requires a payment of $5 per pound as 'technology fee' over and above the price of seed and royalties. If any clause is violated, the grower has to pay one hundred times the damages, and this is not deemed to limit the amount of damages. Monsanto has a right to visit the fields of the farmer for three years after the agreement at any time, even without the farmer being present or taking the farmer's permission. Thus, even the right to property of the farmer is not respected. This clause has made farmers extremely outraged. As one farmer put it, 'We shoot intruders.' The agreement is binding even on heirs and personal representatives or successors of growers, but growers' rights cannot be transferred without Monsanto's permission. Thus, Monsanto's rights exist over others related to the farmer, but the farmer is denied his/her rights to transfer the agreement.

In addition, the agreement has no liability clause. It has no reference to the performance of the seed and Monsanto has no responsibility in case the seed fails to perform as promised or for the ecological damage caused by it. This is especially relevant given the failure of Monsanto's genetically engineered cotton variety, 'Bollgard'. In the 1996 season, farmers ware forced to spray their fields to protect the cotton crop from the Boll worm, even though the promotional material had stated that boll worms could cause no damage to Bollgard cotton.

The Round-Up-Ready Gene Agreement is the latest step in the seed industry's claim for far reaching monopoly rights over seeds and farmers, and bearing no ecological or social responsibility associated with the introduction of herbicide resistant or pest resistant genes into crops. It clearly illustrates the absolute rights of the seed industry and the absolute lack of rights for farmers. This one-sided system in which seed companies have all the rights and bear no social or environmental responsibility and farmers and citizens have no rights, but bear all the risks and costs, can neither protect biodiversity nor provide food security. It is slowly amounting to a system of biodiversity totalitarianism.

Patents on Plants

Patents on plants raise serious concerns about monopolies over food and agriculture systems. There are two trends in plant patents that create a threat to biodiversity, the survival of small farmers, and the food security of all people. The first trend is for broad species patents such as those held by Agracetus (now owned by Monsanto) on cotton and soybean. The granting of patents covering all genetically engineered varieties of a species, irrespective of the genes concerned or how they were transferred, puts in the hands of a single inventor the possibility to control what we grow on our farms and in our gardens.

Unlike plant breeders' rights (PBRs), the utility patents are very broad based, allowing monopoly rights over individual genes and even over characteristics. PBRs do not entail ownership of the germplasm in the seeds, they only grant a monopoly right over the selling and marketing of a specific variety. Patents, on the other hand, allow for multiple claims that may cover not only whole plants, but plant parts and processes as well. So, a company could file for protection of a few varieties of crops, their macro parts (flowers, fruits, seeds and so on), their micro-parts (cells, genes, plasmids and the like) and whatever novel processes it develops to work these parts, all using one multiple claim.

Patent protection implies the exclusion of farmers' right over the resources having these genes and characteristics. This will undermine the very foundations of agriculture. For example, a patent has been granted in the US to a biotechnology company, Sungene, for a sunflower variety with very high oleic acid content. The claim was for the characteristic (i.e., high oleic acid) and not just for the genes producing the characteristic. Sungene has notified others involved in sunflower breeding that the development of any variety high in oleic acid will be considered an infringement of its patent.

The landmark event for the patenting of plants was the 1985 judgement in the US, now famous as exparte Hibberd, in which 'molecular genetics' scientist Kenneth Hibberd and his co-inventors were granted patents on the tissue culture, seed, and whole plant of a corn line selected from tissue culture. The Hibberd application included over 260 separate claims, which give the molecular genetics scientists the right to exclude others from use of all 260 aspects. While Hibberd apparently provides a new legal context for corporate competition, the most profound impact will be felt in the competition between farmers and the seed industry.

A framework is thus now in place that allows the seed industry to realize one of its longest held and most cherished goals—that of forcing all farmers of any crop to buy seed every year instead of obtaining it through reproduction. Industrial patents allow the right to use the product, not to make it. Since seed makes itself, a strong utility patent for seed implies that a farmer purchasing patented seed would have the right to use (or grow) the seed, but not to make seed (to save and replant). If such patents are introduced in India, the farmer who saves and replants the seed of a patented or protected plant variety will be held as violating the law. The US of course is pushing for patent regimes in the area of agriculture in India.

The TRIPs agreement militates against people's human right to food and health by conferring unrestricted monopoly rights to corporations in the vital sectors of health and agriculture. A recent decision on a plant patent infringement suit has set a new precedent for interpreting plant patent coverage in the US where it was ruled that a plant patent can be infringed by a plant that merely has *similar* characteristics to the patented plant. When combined with the reversal of burden of proof clauses, this kind of precedence can be disastrous for countries from where the biodiversity that gave rise to those properties was first taken; more so if the original donors of the biodiversity are accused of 'piracy' through such legal precedence in the absence of the prior existence of biodiversity laws that prevent the misuse of such legal precedence.

In countries, where plant patents are not allowed, patenting genes is available as an opening for patenting properties and characteristics of the plant, and hence having exclusive rights to those properties and characteristics. Further, patents for plant-based products, such as patents for azardirachtin derivative insecticides from the *neem* taken out by transnational corporations like W.R. Grace, will also have a major impact on the access to raw material and market for *neem* products.

In practical terms, allowing patenting in the field of agriculture will have the following adverse consequences:

1. It will encourage monopoly control of plant material by western transnational corporations. This in turn will make farmers dependent on corporations for the most critical

input in agriculture, i.e., seed. This monopoly control is more far-reaching given the takeover of seed companies by large chemical and agribusiness corporations which control other inputs into agriculture such as fertilizers, pesticides and herbicides. Monopoly control on seed linked with corporate control over agriculture will lead to large scale disappearance of farmers' varieties, thus threatening biodiversity conservation as well as farmers' survival. Biodiversity erosion will in turn lead to the erosion of the rich cultural diversity of our country.

2. Due to royalty payments the prices of seeds will go up.

3. The changed economics resulting from IPRs will lead to the displacement of small farmers, who will get into debt and destitution.

4. Large-scale uprooting of agricultural society, without equivalent absorption in new industrial opportunities, will lead to social disintegration, spurt in crime and breakdown of law and order.

5. Intellectual Property protection in the area of agriculture and plant variety will undermine food security since the protected and patented varieties are not linked to food needs, but to the processing and marketing requirements of agribusiness.

6. The shift to control of agriculture through the control of seed will also contribute to secondary impacts on other natural resources, like land and water, getting into the control of MNCs.

7. IPRs in the area of seeds and plants will increase the national debt tenfold. The undermining of food security will increase food imports and hence the foreign exchange burden, thus inviting deeper conditionalities from institutions like the IMF and the World Bank.

8. The erosion of food security will create food dependency,

turning food into a weapon in the hands of industrialized countries, thus leading to total slavery and recolonization.

Patents on Seed: Terminating Germination

Another trend as a result of western-style IPRs is patents for seeds which are sterile or which require the agrichemicals of the same company that has the patent. An example of patents for seed which also force the farmer to buy agrichemicals from the same company are patents for herbicide resistant seeds. Thus, Monsanto's Round-Up-Ready crops are patented and require the purchase of Monsanto's Round-Up Herbicide as well. Round-Up Herbicide is the flagship of Monsanto's agricultural products and of the company overall. According to the company, Round-Up 'destroys every weed, everywhere, economically'. The danger is that Round-Up is a non-selective herbicide, i.e., it does not distinguish between weeds and desirable vegetation, and thus kills all plants, which is in no way 'economical'. In order to gain further monopoly and profits, Monsanto has developed Round-Up Ready crops, which are engineered to be resistant to this lethal Round-Up Herbicide.

Monsanto's patents cover herbicide resistant corn, wheat, rice, soybean, cotton, sugar beet, rapeseed, canola, flax, sunflower, potato, tobacco, alfalfa, poplar, pine, apple and grape. It also covers methods for weed control, planting of seeds, and application of glyphosate. Thus Monsanto controls the entire production process of plants, from the breeding of the plants to their cultivation and sale. While these products would help increase Monsanto's profits, it would destroy diversity and food crops in the Third World and generate artificial demand for unnecessary varieties.

But the real danger in the patenting of seed lies in the Terminator Technology, which has been described as 'the neutron bomb of agriculture'. Terminator Technology was created to prevent farmers from saving non-hybrid, open-pollinated or genetically altered seed sold by seed companies. It began in 1998, when the US Department of Agriculture and the Delta & Pine Land Co., a subsidiary of Monsanto and the largest cotton seed company in the world, announced that they had jointly developed and received a patent on a new, agricultural biotechnology. Benignly titled 'Control of Plant Gene Expression', the new patent permits its owners and licensees to create sterile seed by cleverly and selectively programming a plant's DNA to kill its own embryos. The patent applies to plants and seeds of all species. The result? If saved at harvest for future crops, the seed produced by these plants will not grow. Pea pods, tomatoes, peppers, heads of wheat and ears of corn will essentially become seed morgues. The system has thus been dubbed 'Terminator Technology' and will force farmers to buy seed from seed companies each year.

The US Department of Agriculture and the Delta & Pine Land Co. have applied for patents on the terminator technology in at least seventy-eight countries. What is interesting is that the Department of Agriculture gets a 5 per cent share of profits from the sales, rather astonishing for a government agency. But then, considering the long-term alliance between Monsanto and the USDA, it is not that much of a surprise.

There is another potential dark side to the Terminator. Molecular biologists are examining the risk of the Terminator function escaping the genome of the crops into which it has been intentionally incorporated and moving into surrounding open-pollinated crops or wild, related plants in fields nearby.

Given nature's incredible adaptability and the fact that the technology has never been tested on a large scale, the possibility that the Terminator may spread to surrounding food crops or to the natural environment *must* be taken seriously. The gradual spread of sterility in seeding plants would result in a global catastrophe that could eventually wipe out higher life forms, including humans, from the planet.

These 'gene control' technologies have been rejected by Third World governments and farmers. The only aim of such technology is to force farmers back to the shop every year, and to destroy an age-old practice of local seed-saving that forms the basis of food security in our countries. It will destroy the diversity, the local knowledge and the sustainable agricultural system that our farmers have developed over millennia and undermine our capacity to feed ourselves. IPR regimes based on such technologies view Nature and farmers as 'stealing' seed if farmers use seeds as they were meant to be used—to regenerate the next generation of plants. Rather than stretching a helping hand to farmers, it threatens them with lawsuits and jail.

The implications of gene-control technology such as the Terminator are not just for the farm economy. It will change our very understanding of life and its regeneration, renewal and continuity. Never before has man created such an insidiously dangerous, far-reaching and potentially 'perfect' plan to control the livelihoods, food supply and even survival of all humans on the planet. In one broad, brazen stroke of his hand, man will have irretrievably broken the plant-to-seed-to-plant-to-seed cycle—the cycle that supports most life on the planet. The new technologies and system mean no seed and no food unless you buy more seed.

Instead of removing perversions of US patent law that allow

existing knowledge to be treated as 'novel' and patented, TRIPs has universalized the patenting of life. Patents and property rights on seed imposed through TRIPs are similar to the draconian Salt Laws of the British forbidding the farmer from saving, exchanging and reusing seed from a good harvest. Through the WTO, global corporations like Cargill are putting pressure on India to remove export and import restrictions. Subsidized food imports destroy the livelihoods of millions of farmers. Exports of agricultural producers and changes in the Essential Commodities Act and Public Distribution System are already leading to increase in food prices and increase in hunger and malnutrition. IPRs on seeds will create new economic pressures on farmers and uproot them from their land and livelihoods. Recently, thousands of Indian peasants have committed suicide under the pressure of debt as agrichemical and seed companies, also acting as extension agents and money lenders, trap poor farmers into the purchase of costly seed and pesticide.

In spite of this, new IPR legislation is being introduced in the area of plant genetic resources under pressure of the United States government as well as the requirements of the TRIPs Agreement. Further, the US has been demanding monopoly protection for MNCs which control the seed industry. On the other hand, people's organizations are fighting to protect farmers' rights to their biodiversity and their right to survival, as well as the freedom of scientists to work for the removal of hunger rather than corporate profits. Farmers' organizations, biodiversity conservation groups, sustainable agriculture net-works and public interest oriented scientists are trying to ensure that farmers' rights are protected, and through the protection of farmers' rights, sovereign control over our biological wealth and its sustainable use in agricultural production is ensured. The conflict over plant genetic resource legislation is a conflict between farmers and the seed industry and between the public domain and private profits, between an agriculture that produces and reproduces diversity and one that consumes diversity and produces uniformity.

It is often stated that plant patents will not stop traditional farmers using native seeds. However, when it is recognized that patents are an essential part of a package of agribusiness-controlled agriculture in which farmers no longer use native seeds but seeds supplied by the MNC seed industry, patents become a means of monopoly that wipe out farmers' rights to save and exchange seed. This leads to MNC totalitarianism in agriculture. MNCs will decide what is to be grown by farmers, what they can use as inputs, and when they can sell their produce, to whom and at what price. They will also decide what is to be eaten by consumers, at what price, with what content and how much information is made available to them about the nature of food commodities.

Patents are a significant instrument for the establishment of this form of totalitarianism. The protection of the rights of citizens as producers and consumers needs the forging of new concepts and categories, new instruments and mechanism to counter and limit the monopoly power of MNCs in agriculture. Community rights are an important balancing concept for protecting the public interest in the context of IPR protection for corporations. In the field of food and agriculture, farmers' rights are the countervailing force to breeders' rights and patents on seed and plant material. Farmers' rights in the context of monopoly control of the food system become relevant not just for farming communities, but also consumers. They are necessary not just for the survival of the people but also for the survival of the country. Without sovereign rights of farming communities to their seed and plant genetic resources, there can be no sovereignty of the country.

Farmers' rights are an ecological, economic, cultural and political imperative. Without community rights, agricultural communities cannot protect agricultural biodiversity. This biodiversity is necessary not just for the ecological insurance of agriculture. Rights to agricultural biodiversity is also an economic imperative because without it our farmers and our country will loose their freedom and options for survival. Since biodiversity and cultural diversity are intimately linked, conservation of agricultural biodiversity is a cultural imperative also. Finally, without farmers rights, there is no political mechanism to limit monopolies in agriculture and the inevitable consequences of displacement, hunger and famine that will follow total monopoly control over food production and consumption through monopoly ownership over seed, the first link in the food chain.

Profiteering from Disease

ON 6 MAY 1981, Prime Minister Indira Gandhi, addressing the World Health Assembly in Geneva, said:

> Affluent societies are spending vast sums of money understandably on the search for new products and processes to alleviate suffering and to prolong life. In the process, drug manufacturers have become a powerful industry. My idea of a better-ordered world is one in which medical discoveries would be free of patents and there would be no profiteering from life or death.
>
> —Quoted in B.K. Keayla, *Conquest by Patents*, 1998

The AIDS epidemic has made evident the fact that the cost of health care and drugs is becoming prohibitive in the entire world as a result of implementing US-style patent regimes. Currently there are approximately 32.3 million cases of HIV/AIDS in developing countries. More than 2.5 million people die each year from the disease. While a cocktail of drugs has reduced mortality by 75 per cent and morbidity by 73 per cent over a three-year period in the US, the treatment is costly. Annual treatment costs range between US $10,000 and US $15,000. Even if the UNAIDS initiative subsidised the price by 85 per cent, the cost would be approximately US $2250 per year. And AIDS is only one among other killer diseases like malaria and tuberculosis in the Third World.

In poor countries, drug prices are closely connected to exclusive marketing rights (EMRs) and product patents. Patents preventing generic drug production or cheap imports put drugs beyond the reach of the common people in such countries where GDP per capita ranges from US \$140 to US \$6190. People with AIDS in these countries are thus condemned to premature death. However, with generic drug production, drug prices are lower. As a result of the availability of generic drugs, prices of AIDS drugs in Third World countries are, on the average, 82 per cent lower than prices in the US. The price of treatment also comes down. For example, Flucanazole, a drug used to treat AIDS, is not patented in Thailand. Pfizer was selling the drug for US \$6.2 while the Thai manufacturer priced the drug at US \$0.3, 207 times cheaper than Pfizer. In South Africa, the daily dose of Flucanazole costs US \$21.4 because no generics are available. Two anti-retrovirals cost US \$96 per month in Thailand but US \$342 in Uganda.

Brazil is a country that has made the most progress in producing low cost AIDS medicines. Brazil provides AIDS therapy for US \$192 per month. Starting in 1994, the Brazilian government urged local companies to start making drugs to treat AIDS. The government invoked 'national emergency' provisions in its patent laws to start manufacturing low cost anti-retrovirals such as AZT. Brazil makes eight of the twelve drugs used in the so-called AIDS cocktail. As a result, prices have gone down by more than 70 per cent. The availability of cheaper drugs has enabled the Brazilian government to provide anti-retrovirals to more than 80,000 citizens by the end of 1999, which has led to a more than 50 per cent drop in AIDS related mortality between 1996 and 1999. This has also allowed the government to save US \$472 million in hospitalizations.

However, instead of applauding Brazil for its success in

fighting AIDS through generic drug production supported under its 1997 Patent Law and making this kind of law a model, the US has taken Brazil to the WTO dispute panel in order to force Brazil to undo its patent laws. If US patent monopolies are globalized through TRIPs as a result of being allowed to undo Brazil's patent laws, then millions of AIDS victims in the Third World will be denied affordable treatment and thus their right to life.

In 1977, the South African government also passed a law to provide access to affordable medicines by using the provisions of compulsory licensing and parallel imports. The aim was to reduce the cost of treating HIV/AIDS by 50 to 90 per cent. With over 4 million AIDS patients, the government action was a public health imperative. Yet, all pharmaceutical giants mobilized to challenge the South African law.

Many countries like India have evolved sovereign patent systems which have excluded patents on medicine and food in order to prevent 'profiteering from life and death'. Only process patents on methods of production of pharmaceuticals have been allowed as product patents in sectors such as food and medicine create monopolies, thereby increasing prices in the vital areas of health and nutrition. In India, the 1970 Patent Act was shaped by obligations as laid down in the constitution. After the 1970 Act was enacted, the number of registered pharmaceutical producers (small, medium and large scale) increased from 5,000 to 24,000 with 250 large/medium and 8000 small-scale units. The production of pharmaceutical products also grew forty-eight-fold from Rs 250 crore in 1971 to over Rs 12,068 crore in 1997–98. In a short period of less than ten years, exports increased from Rs 228 crore in 1987–88 to Rs 4090 crore in 1996–97. The multiplicity of producers has been possible because the 1970 Act did not allow product patents in medicine. This competitive environment and exclusion of product patents in medicine has created self-reliance in medicines and kept the prices of medicine within reach of the common man. Prices of medicines in India are in fact much lower than in other countries. The following table shows prices in various countries vis-à-vis India for select medicines.

Differences in Prices of Select Medicines

Drug/Brand	Company	Prices* (in Indian Rupees)				
		India	Pakistan	Indonesia	UK	USA
Ranitidine (Zantac) 150 mg x 10s	Glaxo	7.16	127.08	142.68	339.45	739.60
Times costlier			17.75	19.93	47.41	103.30
Diclofenic (Voltaren) 50 mg x 10s	Ciba Geigy	5.64	69.38	47.96	132.86	505.68
Times costlier			12.30	8.50	23.56	89.66
Piroxicam (Dolonox/Feldene) 20 mg x 10s	Pfizer	24.64	97.23	61.32	254.04	1210.88
Times costlier			3.95	2.49	10.31	49.14

* Retail prices in India and wholesale prices in other countries considered.

Source: Author's research.

Indian medicines are far cheaper than even those in industrialized countries and other developing countries like Pakistan and Indonesia. This is primarily because many developing countries like Pakistan have continued with the colonial 1911 Patent Act inherited from the British which has maintained total dependence on imports with no development in indigenous capacity for production. Given this heavy dependence on imports, MNCs have thus been able to charge higher prices. Efforts of governments to control prices have often effectively been blocked by the MNCs. For example, in 1995, when the Pakistan government imposed a 5 per cent sales tax on drugs and medicine, the MNCs suspended distribution of their products, raising fears of an acute shortage of drugs in the country. The executive director of Pharma Bureau, an association representing multinationals, was quoted in *SCRIP* (9 August 1996) as saying that multinationals will transfer their investments to the Pacific Rim, unless the industry is guaranteed fair and reasonable profit. Pakistan has also been forced to implement the provision of EMRs post the TRIPs agreement. Earlier, the US had taken India to the WTO dispute panel to enforce patent monopolies in pharmaceuticals. Besides India and Brazil, the Dominican Republic, Argentina, Vietnam and Thailand have all been threatened by the US under its Special 301 laws. Challenging the might of the WTO, the US government and pharmaceutical giants, CIPLA, an Indian drug company, announced that it would sell AIDS therapy for $350 a year or less to Medicines Sans Frontiers, which will distribute it for free in Africa. In 2000, Glaxo Wellcome threatened to sue CIPLA when it tried to sell a generic version of a Glaxo anti-AIDS drug combination in Ghana. The African Regional Patent Authority ruled against Glaxo, but CIPLA stopped selling the generic drugs (*The Times of India*, 13 February 2001).

Even industrialized countries have been severely impacted by changes in patent laws, e.g., Canada, although it also has a strong public interest orientation in its health and pharmaceutical policies. In 1994, after the North American Free Trade Agreement (NAFTA) came into force, pharmaceutical plants started to close down. The Canadian trade deficit in pharmaceuticals increased dramatically, reaching $1.6 billion in 1994. As *Drug News and Views* reported in 1995, a major cause for the increasing trade deficit was the fact that brand name companies were closing manufacturing plants in Canada and importing these drugs for sale there.

This pattern of closure of domestic industry and manufacturing capacity and dependence on imports as a result of implementation of US-style patent laws has been repeated in other countries. In Chile, for example, MNCs like Pfizer, Parke-Davis, Squibb, Bayer and Schering have closed manufacturing plants and started importing drugs. This has not only led to job losses but also to steep increases in price. As Myriam Orellana, Executive Director of the Chilean National Industry Association declared, 'The trade benefits and investments which were promised in exchange for the implementation of a US-style patent law have never materialized' (quoted in N. B. Zaveer, *Patents for Medicine*, 1998).

An example of the burden of heavy costs to consumers is the case of Hoffman-La Roche selling its patented products, thorium and valium, to the British National Health Service. Roche Products, a British subsidiary of Hoffman -LaRoche AG, was paying the parent company $925 per kg for one substance that could be bought in Italy for $22.50 per kg, and $2305 per kg for another substance which could be procured in Italy for $50 per kg. The lower prices in Italy were due to the fact that these products were not under patent protection. The Monopolies Commission thus found that Roche Products was overcharging the Health Service. The overcharging amounted to 41 times the cost of alternative supply in the former instance and 46 times in the latter. The government ordered Roche to cut its selling prices for tranquilizers by 60 to 75 per cent and to refund $27.5 million for overcharging.

Patent rights are clearly working against patient rights. The case of AIDS drugs also exposes the myth that product patent regimes help in fighting diseases. By preventing the making of low cost generic drugs, twenty-year patents on drugs can become a cause for the spread of diseases rather than the cure of diseases in the Third World. And patent monopolies prevent low cost medicines from reaching these who need it the most—the poor.

Since patent monopolies lead to higher prices, measures for safeguarding the public interest are very necessary. Such measures include compulsory licenses; licenses of right; automatic lapse; revocation; use and expropriation by the state; provisions against failure to work or insufficient working; and limitations on the importation of the patented articles and on failure to satisfy national market demand. These measures are necessary because in their absence private gain is at public cost. As Surendra Patel observed in his paper 'The Indian Patent Act 1970' presented at the National Seminar of the Patent System in India in 1998, 'the monopolistic privileges granted to the patentees impose heavy cost burdens on the patent-granting countries. They raise the sale prices of the patented products, thereby leading to a forced transfer of income from the consumers to the producers. But these direct costs are only a tip of the iceberg for the developing countries. The indirect or the hidden costs (transfer pricing, abusive practices, limited possibilities of development of national manufacturing) are not figments of academicians' imagination. They are part and parcel of near universal acceptance nowadays.'

Exclusion, rather than compulsory licensing, has been an effective route for the protection of public interest in India. Indian patent law excluded the area of agriculture and horticulture, product patents for medicines, processes for the medicinal, surgical, curative, prophylactic or other treatment of human beings, plants and animals, and atomic energy. It is precisely these safeguards which have been targeted for reversal in the 1990s under the pressure of implementation of the TRIPs agreement and is the most significant issue of public concern in patent law changes in recent times. The pluralistic production base for medicines in India will be totally crippled if the present form of TRIPs is implemented. In addition to paying high prices for pharmaceuticals, the public could end up paying high prices for indigenous medicines as well. In 1998, India was forced to implement EMRs through an amendment of the 1970 Act. However, because of public outrage and a legal challenge in the supreme court by public interest groups, the government has not been able to grant any EMRs. There should thus be no doubt that the pressure to have a globally enforceable uniform patent system is not justified on the basis of empirical evidence of the impact of patents on the public good, especially in the Third World.

Democracy or Dictatorship?

THERE ARE DEEP DIFFERENCES in the positions and attitudes of developed and developing countries to the protection of intellectual property by legislation. Developed countries, and particularly the most industrialized among them, see intellectual property, the fruit of the creative capacity and the intellectual effort of their individual citizens and companies as the legitimate basis for these individuals and companies to earn trading advantage. Such advantage cannot be exercised unless the intellectual property concerned—industrial inventions and discoveries, designs and texts, broadcasts and recordings, trademarks and names showing origin—is given protection against use by others. They believe that in the absence of such protection and the promise of later reward, research and development which leads to inventions and new products of value to all would simply not take place. The latter argument is stated with particular force as a reason to protect the intellectual property of pharmaceutical manufacturers and producers of other goods which take a great deal of money and time to develop, to earn government approval and to bring to market.

Developing countries have a different perspective. They do not, in general, dispute the case for patent and copyright protection. But their individual citizens and companies have little intellectual property of their own to protect, and they do not see reason to give support to international standards of protection that would require them to pay large sums to use technology they needed or which might even deny them access to that technology. Once again, pharmaceuticals and high-technology products are cited as particularly compelling cases, but this time as examples of necessities for national health and development to which access ought not be restricted by high prices enforced through excessive protection of intellectual property.

Thus matters which are of domestic interest to developing countries in terms of right to health and right to development are perceived as issues of trade by northern corporations who are seeking new global markets. Unfortunately, however, national issues of the Third World get converted into global issues for the North in negotiations on intellectual property rights.

Trade Related Intellectual Property Rights (TRIPs)

TRIPs is the international treaty for protecting international property. It is however based on a highly restricted concept of innovation. By definition, it is weighted in favour of transnational corporations and weighted against citizens in general, and Third World peasants and forest dwellers in particular. People everywhere innovate and create. In fact, the poorest have to be most innovative, since they have to work for survival, which is under daily threat. Further, TRIPs is weighted against basic needs and survival and in favour of trade.

In fact, TRIPs was not negotiated by GATT members. It was imposed by MNCs who used the US government to force it on other members. It is the most blatant example of the undemocratic, non-transparent nature of the WTO. The basic framework for the TRIPs patent system was conceived and shaped in a joint statement presented to the GATT Secretariat in June 1988 by the Intellectual Property Committee (IPC) of USA and industry associations of Japan and Europe. IPC is a coalition of thirteen major US corporations dedicated to the finalization of TRIPs in their favour. The members of IPC are corporations like Bristol Myers, Dupont, General Electric, General Motors, Hewlett Packard, IBM, Johnson and Johnson, Merck, Monsanto, Pfizer, Rockwell and Warner.

IPC consulted many interest groups during the whole process. Since no existing trade group or association really filled the bill, they had to create one. Once created, the first task of the IPC was to convince the industrial associations of Europe and Japan that a code was possible. The fundamental principles for protecting all forms of intellectual property was distilled from the laws of the more advanced countries. Besides selling the concepts in the US, IPC went to Geneva to present the document to the staff of the GATT Secretariat and to the Geneva based representatives of a large number of countries.

This was absolutely unprecedented. Industry identified a major problem in international trade, crafted a solution, reduced it to a concrete proposal and sold it to our own and other governments. The industries and traders of world commerce have simultaneously played the role of patients, diagnosticians and prescribing physicians. It is this usurpation of all the roles of the rights of diverse social groups by commercial interests that has led to the displacement of ethical, ecological and social concerns from the substance of the TRIPs agreement. TRIPs has not resulted from democratic negotiations between the larger public and the commercial interests or between industrialized countries and the Third World. It is the imposition of values and interests of northern MNCs on the diverse societies and cultures of the world.

The major thrust for internationalizing IPR laws was thus given by MNCs. Even though IPRs are not a natural right but a statutory right, MNCs have naturalized this right and have used GATT to protect what they have defined as their 'rights' as 'owners of intellectual property'. Since most innovation in the public domain is for domestic, local and public use, not for international trade, TRIPs is only an enforcement of the rights of MNCs to monopolize all production, all distribution and all profits at the cost of all citizens, and small producers worldwide, especially in Third World countries.

Prior to the Uruguay Round, IPRs were not covered by GATT. Each country had its own national IPR laws to suit its ethical and socioeconomic conditions. The most significant change in IPRs through TRIPs was the expansion of the domain of subject matter which is patentable. Article 27.1 of TRIPs on Patentable Subject Matter states that patents shall be available for any inventions, whether products or processes, in all fields of technology, provided that they are new, involve an inventive step and are capable of industrial application.

The removal of all limits on patentability was a demand of the MNCs. This undoes the exclusion in India's patent law, for example, which did not grant patents for food and medicine and allowed only process patents for medicine. The build up of indigenous capacity, the self reliance in medicine, the ability to control prices and keep them low which has been made possible by the 1970 act are all seen by MNCs as loss of profits.

TRIPs has also expanded the scope of patentability to cover life forms. Article 27.5.3(b) of the TRIPs agreement of the WTO refers to the patenting of life. This article enables piracy of indigenous knowledge, and the same interests which see process innovation as involving no inventiveness attempt to claim patents on nature's processes and indigenous knowledge as invention. The Article states, 'Parties may exclude from patentability plants and animals other than micro-organisms, and essentially biological processes for the production of plants or animals other than non-biological and micro-biological processes. However, parties shall provide for the protection of plant varieties either by patents or by an effective *sui generis* system or by any combination thereof. This provision shall be reviewed four years after the entry into force of the Agreement.'

This article forces countries to change patent laws to introduce patents for life forms and introduce plant variety legislation. The first part of the Article addresses the patenting of life. On first reading, it appears that the article is about the exclusion of plants and animals from patentability. However, the words 'other than micro-organisms' and plants and animals produced by 'non-biological' and 'micro-biological' processes make patenting of micro-organisms and genetically engineered plants and animals compulsory.

Since micro-organisms are living organisms, making their patenting compulsory is the beginning of a journey down what has been called the slippery slope that leads to the patenting of all life.

TRIPs and Patents on Plants

The entire structure of patenting of seeds and plants in the US and in TRIPs is based on an arbitrary decision of the US Patent and Trade Mark Office in the Hibberd case in 1985. Prior to this 1985 decision, starting in 1930, the US Congress had granted carefully crafted intellectual property protection for plants. But these laws included important exemptions for farmers and researchers.

The 1985 decision redefined plants as machines and other manufactures, and since then thousands of patents on plants have been given in the US. The US has also pressurized the rest of the world to implement plant patents through TRIPs. The US IPR orthodoxy is based on a fallacious idea that people do not innovate or generate knowledge unless they can derive private profit. However, greed is not a 'fundamental fact of human nature' but a dominant tendency in societies that reward it. In the area of seeds and plant genetic resources, innovation of both the 'formal' and 'informal' systems has so far been guided by the larger human good.

THE UPOV CONVENTION, BREEDERS' RIGHTS AND FARMERS' RIGHTS

The existing international agreement that covers plant breeders' rights is the International Convention for the Protection of New Varieties of Plants—the UPOV Convention. The UPOV Convention was adopted initially by five European countries and membership was restricts to European countries till 1968. At that time the Convention was revised and membership opened to all countries. UPOV was signed in 1961and came into force in 1968. Earlier, the applied version of this Convention was UPOV 1978. Then, a revised version, UPOV 1991, was negotiated and it has come into effect.

UPOV currently has twenty member states including most EC countries, several European countries, Japan, the US and some others. It has no developing country members. It has, therefore, evolved as a legislation suitable to the socioeconomic context of industrialized countries where farmers do not form a large part of the population and do not have any control over plant breeding or seed supply. This situation is very different from contexts like ours where the majority of the population continues to be engaged in farming and farmer's seed production and supply system is still the main source of seed.

The objective of UPOV is to grant certain exclusive rights to plant breeders who develop new varieties of plants.

Normally, farmers provide the source material to the breeders for the development of new varieties. They are also the users of the new varieties developed by the breeders. There is a need for a balance between breeders' rights and what has been called the farmer's privilege.

However, the UPOV Convention is rigid, requiring that members adopt its standards and scope of protection as national law. It has resulted in a high degree of standardization and goes against the reality of biological diversity and the socioeconomic diversity of different countries. It is therefore inappropriate as a *sui generis* system evolved to protect plants, people and creativity in diverse realities.

The standardization is built into the way plant varieties are defined. To be eligible for protection, a variety must be:

New—the variety must not have been exploited commercially.

Distinct—it must be clearly distinguishable from all other varieties known at the date of application for protection.

Uniform—all plants of that particular variety must be sufficiently uniform to allow it to be distinguished from other varieties taking into account the method of reproduction of the species.

Stable—it must be possible for the variety to be reproduced unchanged.

This definition by its very nature rules out farmers' varieties and destroys biodiversity and produces uniformity as necessity. The reward under such a system of Plant Breeders' Rights (PBR) does not go for breeding to maintain and enhance diversity and sustainability, but to the destruction of biodiversity and creating uniform and hence ecologically vulnerable agricultural systems. Therefore, PBR legislation like UPOV is inherently incapable of protecting farmers' rights arising from the role of farmers as breeders who innovate and produce diverse farmers' varieties, which forms the basis for all other breeding systems.

While UPOV fails to recognize and therefore protect farmers' rights as positive rights, UPOV 1978 does have a farmer's exemption which gives the farmer the right to save seed of protected varieties. However, UPOV 1991 has removed these exemptions. Breeders and researchers will have to pay royalty to the PBR holder to use the protected variety for breeding other varieties. It is breeders who will decide their legitimate interests and enforce this on the state. Since breeders are multinational seed companies in this case, more powerful than most Third World governments, 'reasonable limits' will be set by these corporations and not by individual governments. Breeders' authorization will therefore be the final determinant in respect to sale and marketing of harvested material. UPOV 1991 is therefore as monopolistic as patent regimes.

While most Third World governments were not considering the adoption of UPOV 1991, they had an option of joining UPOV 1978 until December 1995. To avoid the more restricted 1991 Convention, most governments were rushing to become members of the 1978 Convention and basing their *sui generis* system on it. Since India did not join UPOV in 1995, if it becomes a member of UPOV now it will have to adopt the 1991 version of the legislation.

Integrity and the intrinsic worth of all species, and the right to life of all, rich and poor alike, calls for an exclusion of life forms from TRIPs and reversal of conventions like UPOV. The review of Article 27.3 (b) in 1999 and the review of the entire TRIPs agreement beginning in 2000 should be used to initiate the exclusion of life forms from patentability so that we can begin the ecological and ethical rehabilitation of all, including humans.

TRIPs and Biodiversity

The Convention on Biological Diversity (CBD) is the international treaty that was signed at the Earth Summit in Rio de Janeiro in 1992. Almost 200 countries are party to the CBD, though seven countries, including the US, have not ratified it. The TRIPs agreement which has expanded patents to cover life forms undermines the potential and promises of the Convention on Biological Diversity. Since individual countries which are members of both treaties have to implement both of them, the conflicts between CBD and TRIPs has serious problems for implementation.

The CBD is a legally binding agreement for the conservation of biological diversity, the sustainable use of its components and the fair and equitable sharing of the benefits arising from the utilization of genetic resources, including through appropriate access to genetic resources and by appropriate transfer of relevant technologies. These objectives of conservation, sustainable utilization and equitable benefit sharing are all undermined by the TRIPs agreement. TRIPs prevents government action for sharing the benefits of the use of biodiversity and ensuring such utilization is sustainable and conserves biodiversity in an equitable manner since it obliges states to protect patent monopolies. For most people, sharing biological heritage is the only legitimate way of sharing benefits equitably. By making such sharing and exchange illegal, western-style patent systems undermine the very basis of equitable benefit sharing.

A patent gives the patent holder the right to exclude others from taking commercial and economic advantage of his patented 'invention' for the life of the patent, which under TRIPs is twenty years. It gives the patentee the right to restrain any other person from manufacturing, importing, selling or using such patented article or patented process.

When the patented 'invention' is a life form, or a part or product of a biological resource, patent rights give the patent holder, which is usually a corporation, the right to prevent farmers from saving seed, small manufacturing units from making products based on biodiversity using processes which have been pirated from indigenous cultures (e.g. W.R. Grace's patents for making *neem* pesticides and fungicides). Hence TRIPs undermines the very objective of CBD.

Another important aspect of CBD is the principle of sovereignty. The Convention recognizes the sovereign rights of states over their biological and genetic resources. This sovereignty includes shaping regimes of property rights to biodiversity. On the other hand, the patents on life clause of TRIPs defines life forms as 'intellectual property' and hence creates a global private property rights regime by undermining the sovereignty of states to shape and evolve their own IPR systems.

CBD also requires signatories to protect and promote the rights of communities, farmers and indigenous peoples vis-à-vis their customary use of biological resources and knowledge systems. CBD requires the protection of indigenous knowledge on the other hand, TRIPs, based on western-style patent systems has no system for recognizing or protecting indigenous knowledge. Hence it promotes biopiracy.

Since these issues of sovereignty conservation, sustainable utilization, equitable sharing of benefits and protection of indigenous knowledge are so important for Third World countries which are rich in biodiversity and where people's livelihoods are dependent on biodiversity, these countries have repeatedly made appeals for the primacy of CBD over TRIPs.

TRIPs is based on private rights, CBD is based on the

principle of sovereignty. TRIPs has no conservation obligation, CBD has the obligation to conserve biodiversity and indigenous knowledge. These inconsistencies need to be removed so that countries can implement coherent laws at national level to protect the environment and ensure people's needs are met and their rights are protected. CBD should be treated as the higher international law since it is about the higher values and larger good, and the review of TRIPs should ensure that changes are made in TRIPs to make TRIPs consistent with CBD.

TRIPs and Patent Laws in India

Patent laws were first introduced in India in the 1850s as part of colonial rule. In 1911, the first Patent Act was enacted. The 1911 Act was the law in force at the time of independence. It was amended in 1930 and 1945. In 1970 a new Patent Act was enacted, shaped by 22 years of debate, discussion and review (see Appendix).

The central debates at the time of independence and after fifty years of independence remain the same—the question of monopolies and the stifling of societal creativity and indigenous production. The most significant contribution of the 1970 Act is to have prevented monopolies in the vital areas of health and nutrition by excluding food and medicine from product patents. Exclusion, rather than compulsory licensing, seems to have been the more effective route for protection of the public interest. However, it is precisely these safeguards that affect the daily life of Indian citizens which have been targeted for dismantling in the 1990s under the pressure of the implementation of the TRIPs agreement.

In spite of the failure of the Seattle Round of WTO, the Government of India rushed in a series of Intellectual Property

Right (IPR) related legislations in December 1999 on grounds that these were needed to implement TRIPs by 1 January 2000.These IPR legislations include:

1. The Protection of Plant Varieties and Farmers' Rights Bill, 1999
2. The Patent (Amendment) Act, 1999
3. The Trade Marks Bill, 1999
4. The Copyrights Bill, 1999
5. The Geographical Indications and Marks (Registration and Protection) Bill, 1999
6. The Design Act, 1999

THE PATENT (AMENDMENT) ACT, 1999

The main objective of the Patent (Amendment) Act, 1999 is to remove exclusion of product patents in the areas of food, medicine and drugs. According to the government, this has been necessitated by India's obligations as a signatory to the WTO. However, by merely introducing new clauses for exclusive marketing rights associated with product patent applications in the area of pharmaceuticals and agrichemicals as required by the TRIPs treaty without introducing new clauses for exclusion, the Patent (Amendment) Act, 1999, in fact, opens the floodgates to:

1. Patenting of life forms
2. Patenting of products derived from living organisms
3. Patenting of genes, components and parts of living organisms.

The Indian Patent Act, 1970, had excluded large areas from patentability. The 1999 Act in contrast gives Exclusive Marketing Rights (EMRs) merely on the basis of foreign patents obtained after 1 January 1995 without any scrutiny on the basis of impact on public health, public morality, or the public interest. Since many patents held in foreign countries are based on the piracy of indigenous knowledge (e.g., use of *neem*, pepper, ginger, etc.) or are based on patents on life (e.g., patents on human cell lines, blood from the umblical cord, patents on animals and plants), granting EMRs on the basis of such patents without establishing criteria and rules for exclusion amounts to unleashing market forces which will destroy our economic base, our environment, our public health and even the ethical fabric of our society.

Adding to the concern is the fact that the 1999 Patent (Amendment) Act has failed to use any of the safeguards TRIPs allows. For example, TRIPs enables countries to exclude patents on life since such patents violate our public morality. While allowing product patents for medicines and drugs, and granting EMRs on the basis of such patent applications, the Patent (Amendment) Act should also have introduced an exclusion clause reflecting our rights under Article 27.2 of TRIPs.

It is only in the Patent (Amendment) Act that the exclusions from patentability can be established and the public interest and public morality protected. Accordingly, given the new phenomena of patents on animals, plants and even human cell lines, and the new epidemic of biopiracy and the patenting of our indigenous knowledge, an exclusion clause is an imperative from the ethical, ecological and economic perspective. A failure to clearly spell out what products will not be patentable, and hence what products will not be eligible for EMRs, is necessary for the protection of the *ordre public* and the livelihoods and basic needs of the Indian people who depend on access to biodiversity and its products for their survival.

The Patent (Amendment) Act has also failed to create legal

instruments to stop biopiracy. It does not establish criteria for non-patentability of indigenous knowledge, it merely refers to the right to sell or distribute such products. In substances or products it only refers to Indian medicine and leaves out indigenous medicine or practices. This has also been pointed out in the Law Commission Report. Since most biopiracy patents are based on trivial modifications in methods of extraction or use, it is necessary to amend Article 3 of the Patent Act which specifies what will not be counted as an invention.

The most serious loophole in the Patent (Amendment) Act is that while exclusive marketing rights are offered to corporations without any exemptions and exclusions, no safeguards have been put in place for protecting the public interest. Sections 24(c) and 24(d) create the illusion of compulsory licensing. However, compulsory licensing only applies to production and manufacture and is meaningless in the context of selling and distribution. Similarly, price control can only be applied if a product is produced domestically. Price controls and compulsory licensing are not applicable for EMRs. The Patent (Amendment) Act has thus created absolute unregulated marketing rights for global corporations and undermined the rights of the Indian people to adequate and accessible nutrition and health care.

There are thus two main inadequacies in the 1999 Act. Firstly, by merely adding new clauses that give unlimited powers to corporations, particularly transnational corporations in the areas of health and agriculture, the bill totally undermines the public interest and the national interest that was structured into the 1970 Act. Secondly, by making amendments to allow for a selective implementation of TRIPs which only reflect the increased powers and rights of corporations without commensurate amendments to implement those clauses of

TRIPs that can empower the state to protect the public interest, the Patent (Amendment) Act has, in fact, reduced the state to merely being an instrument of transnational corporations and not a protector of the Indian public and their interests.

Even the TRIPs agreement, which has in fact been drafted by the pharmaceutical and biotechnological industry, has been forced to recognize that the new powers being given to the private interest will create the need for governments to step in, to draw boundaries, and put limits on patents in order to protect public interest and preserve the moral fabric of society as well as protect the health of plants, animals and humans and the environment. Articles 7 and 8 of TRIPs allow for evolving appropriate instruments in national legislations to protect public interest. The Patent (Amendment) Act however has no clauses that reflect the possible options that the Government of India has through these Articles to protect the public interest in the context of the expanded scope of product patents into areas which the 1970 Act had prohibited. And given the new powers made available to corporate and private interests through the Patent (Amendment) Act and taking into account the emergence of new technology and IPR regimes, the absence of clear definitions as well as the absence of articulation of sharp and new criteria for defining exclusions of subject matter on ethical, ecological and economic grounds amounts to a total surrender of the public interest and national interest to global commercial interests.

The 1970 Act had a number of mechanisms for ensuring technology transfer. These included compulsory licensing, as well as the need for 'working the patent' in India. This was necessary because multinationals often take patents in Third World countries and do not work their patents there, with the intention of preventing others from using the innovation. A WIPO/UNCTAD study shows that less than 5 per cent of foreign-owned product patents in Third World countries were actually used to protect production processes in those countries. The Patent (Amendment) Act will, in fact, ensure that such import monopolies are created, because it has totally undone the objective of Section 83 of the 1970 Act which tried to ensure that inventions were commercially worked in India. In addition, the 1970 Act gave the government the powers to allow compulsory licensing and licenses of rights and revocations on grounds of public interest and reasonable pricing through Sections 84–90. These sections of the 1970 Act ensured technology transfer and prevented import monopolies. The public interest served through these clauses has been undermined through Amendment 24 (c) of the proposed Bill, which states that 'working of the invention shall be deemed to be selling or distributing of the article or substance'.

The Patent (Amendment) Act as it stands will undermine people's health dramatically through a complex set of interlinked mechanisms. Unrestricted patents will allow patenting of medicinal plants and drugs used in indigenous medical systems by transnational pharmaceutical corporations. Seventy per cent of health care is still accounted for by indigenous systems because they are accessible to due to their low cost. Patents on traditional knowledge and medicinal plants by transnational corporations will immediately take these health care systems beyond the reach of the majority of the Indian people. The introduction of product patents in the area of medicines will prevent Indian companies from using other processes to manufacture drugs at lower costs than those of global corporations. Drug prices, particularly of life saving drugs, will rise dramatically and go beyond people's reach.

Patents on diagnostics, when combined with increased privatization of health care under structural adjustment programmes, take tests and diagnosis beyond the reach of the people.

Patents on life forms unrestricted by health concerns will lead to new health hazards as a consequence of releasing robust genetically engineered organisms into the environment both in agriculture and in medicine.

The 1970 Act excluded all methods of agriculture and horticulture from patentability. In addition, the exclusion of product patents in the area of agrichemicals was also ensured through Section 5a. The Patent (Amendment) Act ,1999 removes these restrictions in the field of agriculture. The removal of exclusions on patents in the field of agriculture will undermine the nutritional status of the people by increasing the costs of food production.

Further, since it does not articulate new demarcation criteria for exclusions, it allows the patenting of plants, plant products, plant characteristics, their genes, biopesticides, biofertilizers, etc. The totally unrestricted scope of patenting in agriculture that the 1999 Act leads to will undermine Indian agriculture, threaten Indian farmers and imperil food security.

Therefore, major amendments are needed that categorically exclude:

1. Patents on life forms
2. Patents on naturally occurring substances
3. Patents on genes, components and parts of living organisms.

These amendments, based on clear articulation of exclusions in the new areas of product patents are both ethically and economically necessary, as well as realistically achievable in the existing world situation. Further, since the exclusion of the Patent Act of 1970 are being undone under the current legislation, a special clause is needed for public opposition to exclusive marketing rights that will for all practical purposes function as product patents to ensure that the moral order and the environment are protected.

INDIA JOINS THE PARIS CONVENTION: TRIPS THROUGH THE BACK DOOR

Patent politics in India started more than a decade ago with a rejection of the pressure being put on India to join the Paris Convention by industrially advanced countries. Everyone knew that the costs of joining the Paris Convention were much higher than the benefits to be derived from it. The campaign to stay out of the Paris Convention then became the National Campaign against the change of India's patent laws and ultimately the campaign against TRIPs.

The WTO dispute ruling against India on the implementation of Articles 70.8 and 70.9 of TRIPs however created new pressure for amending India's Patent Act. However, it was not proving to be easy to change a system designed for our socioeconomic conditions without major resistance.

The announcement of India joining the Paris Convention is in fact a back door entry for TRIPs. All references to the Paris Convention exaggerate the benefits for India by treating all enterpreneurs as 'inventors' and making it appear as if being part of a Patent Cooperation Treaty (PCT) under the Convention will bring benefits to our industrialists. The people of India, of course, count for nothing in the worldview of those defending India's joining of the Paris Convention. People's intellectual rights to their knowledge and their economic rights to seed, food and medicine at accessible prices can be totally extinguished according to them.

The Indian experience on the implementation of the TRIPs Agreement has made it evident that the IPR regimes embodied in TRIPs necessitate the bypassing of the democratic process. The debate is growing between those who support the democratic choice of nationally suited and independently evolved patent regimes and those who opt for the authoritarian imposition of universalized patent systems evolved by MNCs and pushed by the governments of industrialized countries in the Uruguay Round of GATT.

This debate is however not limited to India. It is taking place within the WTO itself where the Trade and Environment Committee is looking at the environmental implications of TRIPs. When the articles relevant to biological organisms and life forms came up for review in 1999, the debate on the ethical, ecological and democratic implications of patents on life will have deepened and widened.

The Way Forward

CURRENTLY, WELL OVER 190 genetically engineered animals, including fish, cows, mice and pigs are figuratively standing in line to be patented by researchers and corporations. It is this inexorable rush for patenting all life forms and their parts that will be extended through the global implementation of TRIPs in its present draft which will restrict systems of recognition of innovation and access to knowledge.

The first restriction is the shift from common rights to private rights. As the preamble of the TRIPs agreement states, intellectual property rights are recognized only as private rights. This excludes all kinds of knowledge, ideas and innovations that take place in the 'intellectual commons'—in villages among farmers, in forests among tribals and even in universities among scientists. TRIPs is therefore a mechanism for the privatization of the intellectual commons and a de-intellectu-alization of civil society, so that the mind becomes a corporate monopoly.

The second restriction of intellectual property rights is that they are recognized only when knowledge and innovation generate profits, not when they meet social needs. Article 27.1 of TRIPs refers to the condition that to be recognized as an IPR, innovation has to be capable of industrial application. This immediately excludes all sectors that produce and innovate outside the industrial mode of organization of production.

Profits and capital accumulation are recognized as the only ends to which creativity is put. The social good is no longer recognized. Under corporate control a 'de-industrialization' of production in the small scale and in the informal sectors of society takes place.

However, TRIPs is not just about trade. It is also about the ethics of how we relate to other species and what we hold as the moral and cultural values of our civilization. It is about how our biodiversity is used and controlled—by local communities who have protected it, or by corporations, which have found new ways to exploit and own it. It is an issue of justice and human rights. Since it robs people of their right to livelihoods and right to meet basic needs, it is a tragedy that an issue directly related to the economic, ecological and ethical fabric of our society, and to the economic options of survival of our people should be left to MNCs and trade bureaucrats. In Indian culture life cannot be patented because it cannot be owned and it is not manufactured. TRIPs force us to give up such moral values, economic priorities and sovereignty.

TRIPs has also forced countries to grant both product and process patents for all products. The TRIPs agreement has, therefore, undone the strength of individual country patent laws, such as that of India which ensured people had access to food and medicine by excluding food and medicine from patentability. The TRIPs agreement makes it obligatory on members to make patents available to all inventions. The conditions for patentability are novelty and non-obviousness and utility, i.e., it should not have been invented earlier by anybody else, it should be new in a non-obvious way and it should be capable of industrial application.

Further, TRIPs has removed the distinction between local

production and imports, which was an essential element of the 1970 Patent Act of India. The 1970 Act had the clear objective to ensure that patents 'are not granted merely to enable patentees to enjoy a monopoly for the importation of the patented article'. Article 27.1 of TRIPs has undone the 1970 safeguard to prevent monopolies by stating that 'patent rights shall be enjoyable without discrimination as to the place of invention, the field of technology and whether products are imported or locally produced'. By treating import monopolies as a 'discrimination', the TRIPs agreement has brought patent laws back to the colonial pattern in which colonies were made dependent on imported goods and local production and manufacture was dismantled.

TRIPs Reform and Review

According to the transitional arrangement, developing countries were expected to implement TRIPs by 1 January 2000. Least Developed Countries can implement TRIPs by 1 January 2005. Developing countries also have time upto 1 January 2005 to introduce product patents in areas of technology which were not protected by product patents, such as drugs and pharmaceuticals in India under the 1970 Patent Act. However, before the period of transitional arrangements expires, WTO members are supposed to undertake a review. Implementation can be frozen while this review is being undertaken.

If measures for safeguarding the public interest were not in place, patent regimes would increase private gain at public cost. Exclusion of subject matter from patentability is one means of protecting the public interest. But most important is review and changes in TRIPs and individual country laws. A review process therefore needs to be put in place, which is informed by new developments in a democratic and transparent way. Four important new developments have emerged since the signing of TRIPs:

1. The epidemic of biopiracy, i.e., the patenting of indigenous knowledge.
2. Emergence of new technologies such as the Terminator Technology and hazardous genetic engineering.
3. Emergence of monopolies in the form of major life sciences corporations.
4. Emergence of broad based citizen movements against patents on life.

Since the very objectives of the Agreement are being undermined by these new developments, a substantive review must begin at the earliest. Till then there is no necessity for developing countries to be bullied into implementing TRIPs.

The protection and enforcement of intellectual property rights should contribute to the promotion of technological innovation and to the transfer and dissemination of technology, to the mutual advantage of producers and uses of technological knowledge, and in a manner conducive to social and economic welfare, and to a balance of rights and obligations. Patents based on biopiracy, patents for technologies like Terminator Technology and the concentration of the life sciences industry undermines all aspects of the objectives of TRIPs. Biopiracy blocks the transfer and dissemination of technology, Patents for terminator-like technologies work against farmers and food security. Patents on biological processes and products are not conducive to the social and economic welfare of the poor since they take vital resources beyond their access. Patents on life forms also create an imbalance of rights and obligations. All over the world citizens are organizing to stop patents on life and monopolies on life. In Austria and Switzerland citizens organized referendums on issues of patents on life. Citizens are asking for life forms and biodiversity to be fully excluded from TRIPs. These new democratic developments on decisions related to patents should inform the review, substance and implementation of TRIPs.

There are arguments for a freeze on implementation and pushing back the implementation period to 1 Janaury2005 as well. Firstly, it is reasonable and rational to implement the agreement <u>after</u> the review process, not before the review. Secondly, the present transitional arrangements require developing countries to change IPR laws three times in 10 years. This creates judicial chaos and adds administrative and legislative burdens on already stretched resources. Conficts between citizens and government, between the public interest and the corporate interest can be avoided if the implementation of TRIPs is frozen while democratic debates are initiated and a review of TRIPs is started, and TRIPs is amended to ensure a balance of corporate rights and responsibilities. A third reason why a TRIPs review is imperative is that there is a major conflict between the Convention and Biological Diversity (CBD) and TRIPs, an issue already brought to the WTO by India's submission.

The citizen agenda for the TRIPs review is therefore 'first review, then implement'. In specific terms, this agenda implies:

1. WTO members should begin the review of Art 27.3 (b) immediately.
2. The TRIPs council should undertake a substantive review of TRIPs in the light of new developments at the earliest.
3. Democratic debates should be initiated in parliaments and society on patents on life, the balance between rights and responsibility of corporations, governments and citizens, resolution of conflicts between trade interests and conservation

interests. These democratic debates should improve the review process.

4. There should be a freeze on the implementation of TRIPs for five years while the debates and reviews are undertaken.

5. All aspects of TRIPs which go counter to CBD obligations should be amended so that the objectives of CBD are not undermined.

6. To maintain the balance of rights and responsibility in the area of biotechnology, a strong Biosafety Protocol should be put in place before countries are required to implement TRIPs.

When TRIPs was forced on countries during the Uruguay Round, many issues of public concern were totally bypassed and the full ethical, ecological and economic implications of patenting life were not discussed. Third World countries were coerced into accepting that western-style IPR systems were 'strong' and 'advanced'. However, public interest groups showed that these systems were strong to establish corporate monopolies globally, but they were weak to protect indigenous knowledge and prevent biopiracy. They were 'advanced' means for taking away the resources of the poor, and stealing the knowledge of our grandmothers. But they were primitive when viewed from the perspective of justice, equality and cross-cultural respect.

As a result of sustained public pressure, after the agreement came into force in 1995, many Third World countries have made their recommendations for changes in Article 27.3 (b) to prevent biopiracy. Clearly there is a case for re-examining the need to grant patents on life forms anywhere in the world. Till such systems are in place, it may advisable to:

1. Exclude patents on all life forms.

If this is not possible then,

2. Exclude patents based on traditional/indigenous knowledge and essentially derived products and processes from such knowledge, or at least

3. Insist on disclosure of the country of origin of the biological source and associated knowledge, and obtain consent of the country providing the resource and knowledge, to ensure equitable sharing of benefits.

Instead of recognizing that it is promoting piracy and changing its laws to prevent its practice, the US has rejected all Third World proposals for the recognition and protection of indigenous knowledge. On the issue of biopiracy, the US states that the requirement to patent applicants to identify in their application the source of any genetic materials or traditional knowledge used in developing their claim 'would be impractical'. Recognizing and screening indigenous knowledge should be a necessary element of the test for inventiveness and novelty that is required under any patent system. However, when it comes to traditional knowledge of the Third World, this screening for *prior art* is declared as impractical. Forcing all countries to change their patent laws in spite of protests is considered practical. Imposing an immoral order of patents on life in spite of people in the North and South not accepting patents on life is considered practical. Changing all cultures of the world, and enforcing property rights on seed is considered practical. Collecting royalties from the poor in the Third World for resources and knowledge that came from them in the first place is considered practical. But taking the simple step to change one clause in one law in the US and one clause in TRIPs is considered impractical. This suggests that the US is committed to not taking any steps to prevent Biopiracy, and is in fact committed to promoting it.

TRIPs and US-style patent laws annihilate rights of Third World communities by not having any system of recognition and protection of indigenous knowledge and not having any system for preventing patents claiming piracy of such knowledge as an invention.

The US proposes that the Third World should solve the problem of biopiracy by granting access to the companies which are patenting indigenous knowledge. Instead of correcting the deficiencies in TRIPs and US-style patent laws, the US would like to maintain the structures and laws that promote biopiracy at the global level. Instead of changing the laws at the international level and in the US which allow pirated knowledge to be treated as an 'invention', the US wants the Third World to write contracts with the 'biopirates'.

Farmers Rights as Community Rights: The *Sui Generis* System

The first part of Article 27.3 (b) of TRIPs requires that parties allow patenting of plants and animals produced through 'non-biological' and 'microbiological processes'. The reference is quite evidently to the new biotechnologies of genetic engineering. However, while the moving of species across species barriers through genetic engineering techniques can be defined as 'non-biological' in the sense that such mixing of genetic material would not happen in nature, the 'production' of plants and animals with genes introduced from other species takes place essentially through the biological process of reproduction.

While patenting of plants and animals has become prevalent in the US and UK, the article in TRIPs governing patenting of plants and animals creates major problems that will need to be reviewed. It would, therefore, be more useful for developing countries to wait for the TRIPs review before changing their patent regimes.

The second part of Article 27.5.3(b) of TRIPs states that parties shall provide for the protection of plant varieties either by patents or by an effective *sui generis* system or by any combination thereof. This provision shall be reviewed four years after the entry into force of the Agreement.

This is the part that will most directly affect farmers' rights as innovators and plant breeders, and their community ownership of seed and plant material. TRIPs recognizes only the western industrialized model of innovation and has failed to recognize the more informal, communal system of innovation through which Third World farmers produce, select, improve and breed a plethora of diverse crop varieties. Farmer's seeds reflect the ingenuity, inventiveness and genius of our people. However, the protection of the collective intellectual property of Third World farmers does not even find a place in TRIPs.

While the phrase *sui generis* gives the impression that each country is free to set up its own IPR system, the key term is 'effective', which makes the adoption of a global regime necessary. This word was inserted by the US in the Biodiversity Convention and in the TRIPs Agreement. The first sentence of that draft refers to the need to 'promote' effective and adequate protection of intellectual property rights. The same phrase is in Section 301 of the Trade and Competitiveness Act of 1988, which has been used to retaliate against countries whose IPR laws do not conform to US standards.

The use of the term 'effective' in all negotiations related to IPRs and biodiversity is a result of US attempts to globalize its IPR regimes. In the Dunkel text, the phrase 'effective *sui generis* system' implies that such a system will not be determined by countries but by GATT. Further, given the trend of developments in international negotiations, the only system recognized as 'effective' at the international level is the system of plant breeders' rights as codified in UPOV. Thus, whether it is patents or an 'effective' *sui generis* system, both systems threaten farmers' rights, unless we interpret *sui generis* as sovereign and create *sui generis* systems which are alternatives to UPOV.

The ecological vulnerability of agricultural monocultures has made the conservation of agricultural biodiversity an environmental imperative. The Convention on Biodiversity Conservation (CBD) has been one of the responses of the world community to conserve the ecological basis of biological production through biodiversity conservation. There is ample legal ground to go beyond UPOV in evolving a *sui generis* framework for protecting biodiversity, including plant diversity, especially in light of CBD. It is also an imperative because without it we will not be able to protect community intellectual rights.

There are two new political conditions that the CBD has given rise to. Firstly, it has recognized the national sovereign right of countries to their biological wealth. Secondly, it has recognized the contribution of indigenous communities to knowledge about the utilization of biodiversity. Recognition of sovereignty and indigenous knowledge creates a major shift in the political context of the ownership, use and control of genetic resources, especially in the area of agricultural biodiversity, including seeds and plant genetic resources. The seeds of the Third World can no longer be treated as the 'common heritage of mankind', freely accessible to all, including western seed corporations. The seeds sold by transnational seed corporations can no longer be regarded as the only ones embodying an intellectual contribution. Seeds saved by farmers also embody significant intellectual contribution. A third major shift in recent years has been the recognition that 'improvement' of seed is not absolute and context independent. Improvement is a contextual category. 'Improvement' of crops can also be from the view of farmers. Thus, agribusiness 'improves' crops for industrial processing, or for increased use of chemical inputs, whereas farmers need crops which are easy to process at home and crops that decrease the dependence on external inputs.

Conventional breeding only looks at yield potential and yield potential is defined as 'the yield of a crop when growth is not limited by water or nutrients, pests, diseases or weeds'. In the realities of farmers' fields, these are precisely the limitations that farmers face, and their breeding is responsive to the environmental stress and ecological diversity within which they must practice the agriculture. Corporate breeding strategies therefore cannot be treated as the only direction of evolution in breeding and research, and 'improvement' from the perspective of MNC interests cannot be translated into an overall societal benefit. Monopoly by MNCs in seed through IPRs is therefore neither desirable nor necessary from the public interest perspective.

That is why we need to question the assumptions that the Government of India should produce legislation to protect US seed corporations so that they can provide the 'best seeds for Indian farmers'. What is good for Pepsi and Cargill and Monsanto and Pioneer is not necessarily good for Indian farmers and Indian consumers. Pepsi needs tomatoes and potatoes for processing into tomato ketchup and potato chips for its fast food chains like KFC and Pizza Hut. Cargill needs sorghum and maize for its feed industry. Monsanto is interested in selling more of its herbicide through herbicide resistant rape-seed. These are not the characteristics of seed that Indian farmers would choose in their breeding strategies or characteristics of food that Indian consumers would choose for cooking qualities in their diverse food systems.

Farmers' rights reflect the recognition of sovereignty in ownership and creativity in traditional breeding by farmers as well as alternative breeding strategies for protection of the biodiversity base of agriculture. Without farmers' rights, Third World countries cannot assert their sovereign rights to their agricultural biodiversity or in their agricultural policy. Further, without the ownership rights of farming communities, biodiversity cannot be conserved.

No model yet exists which recognizes these rights of farmers and other producer communities who derive their livelihood from biodiversities. The rights of farmers, tribals, pastoralists, herbalists and fisherfolk to the biodiversity that they have conserved and used from time immemorial can be effectively granted only if they are allowed to participate actively in decisions that have an impact on the status of their rights and the status of biodiversity. It is to fill this gap that we need a concept of farmers' rights as a sub-category of community rights. On the one hand, community rights recognize the creativity and protect the livelihoods of diverse communities. On the other hand, they set limits and boundaries on the domain of monopoly protection shaped by IPRs. In the case of agricultural biodiversity, these community rights are farmers' rights. They should recognize the creativity of farmers, protect farmers' livelihoods and resist IPR monopolies.

The dominant model of free unprotected flow of knowledge and resources from the gene rich south to the capital rich north and the protected flow of knowledge and resources in the reverse direction is brazenly unjust and non-sustainable and needs to be changed. It can only change through a political process which recognizes the original contributors of knowledge and genetic resources and respects their value system. Community rights are a balancing mechanism for IPRs as a part of building such a political process. A world in which market values are the only values will impoverish us all—nature, the Third World and the international community. To keep non-market, non-monetary systems of value and systems of biodiversity and knowledge alive and to subject the logic of the market to these higher value systems is the real political task for establishing rights to knowledge and biological resources.

People's contribution to the development of an adequate *sui generis* system for plants should therefore focus on the three imperatives of ethics and ecology, recognition of creativity by communities, and economic equity.

1. *The ethical and ecological imperative to recognize the intrinsic worth of all species*—Countries need to have strong legislation to allow exclusion of patents on life on grounds of public morality. This is a possibility allowed in Article 25 of the TRIPs agreement. Areas excluded from patentability need to be governed by non-monopoly regimes which protect peoples' rights to creativity and innovation.

2. *The imperative for equal recognition of creativity in diverse cultures*—Diverse cultures have evolved different traditions of knowledge and innovation which need to be treated with equal respect and significance. This is also needed for cultural diversity. In the area of biodiversity, indigenous knowledge of farmers, tribals and herbals is the primary source of knowledge of properties of plants. A *sui generis* system thus needs to recognize this indigenous innovation, even though in structure, process and motivation it differs

from the innovation in industrial systems. Through this recognition it should prevent the piracy of indigenous knowledge and of the biodiversity in which it is embodied. Community rights or farmers rights as collective intellectual rights therefore need to be evolved.

3. *The economic imperative to provide all members of societies with health and nutrition*—Monopolies in areas crucial to survival have been prevented through various mechanisms. Thus, because food and health are central to survival, national patent laws have prevented the monopolization of patents in these areas. For example, the Indian Patent law does not allow patents for living resources.

The existing legal framework for intellectual property rights recognizes only the northern industrial model of innovation. It has failed to recognize the more informal, communal system of innovation through which southern farmers and indigenous communities produce, select, improve and breed a diversity of crop and livestock varieties, often over a long period of time. Essentially this is a clash of the definition of knowledge systems. It is therefore proposed to define 'innovation' which recognizes the *collective* and *cumulative* intellectual right of such communities as a corollary to perfecting it. Additionally, the definition recognizes such knowledge howsoever recorded, whether formally or informally (orally, anecdotal, etc.). This is to take account of communities in the Third World who may not have a written tradition or culture.

The word 'property' has been designed to exclude knowledge systems of communities. Property rights in the term 'intellectual property rights', as presently understood, connotes commoditization and ownership in private hands primarily for commercial exchange. The relationship of a community to its knowledge is integrally uncommoditized and communally 'owned' and shared. The sum total of communally-owned knowledge which is of value (though not necessarily priced) is then more aptly described by the term 'community intellectual rights'.

It is also suggested that governments exercise their sovereign rights over genetic diversity jointly with the owners of that diversity, i.e., the farming communities, to prevent piracy of genetic material, to strengthen the negotiating capacity of the country by having state sovereignty backed by people's sovereignty, and to ensure just returns for allowing access to genetic material. In order to protect farmers' rights, it is essential that access to such genetic material be made conditional to negotiations between the parties interested in acquiring the material and the communities concerned and their governments.

Farmers' varieties need to be protected because they are perennial and perpetual and always useful, in contrast to breeders' varieties, whose usefulness is time bound. It is necessary to ensure that the right exists in perpetuity and cannot be extinguished. Such a prohibition to advance public policy is common in domestic legislation. Farmers have a right to the continuation of free exchange and access emanating from whole communities to other reciprocating communities. It is predicated upon the non-exclusive holding of common knowledge, innovations and practices of indigenous and local communities in respect of genetic resources and biological diversity. The free sharing does not apply if there is commercial utilization of the variety or innovation. It should be assured that communities retain control over their resources, emphasizing the non-monopolistic facet of community innovation.

To prevent prolonged dispute as to whether the variety, knowledge, practice or technology relating to the innovation is in the custodianship of a community, a declaration by the duly constituted representatives of the community that they have been using the variety or innovation or are the custodians of the variety or innovation should suffice. In some cases, more than one community may have contemporaneously created the genetic resource and the technologies or accumulated the knowledge. The innovation will, in such circumstances, vest jointly in all these communities and each will have complete rights and duties in relation to it and any payments will be apportioned accordingly. Often, communities may be weak in enforcing their rights and give charge to the state to protect its interests in negotiations for access with foreign/commercial companies. As this obligation of the state emerges from joint ownership with communities, the state cannot take unilateral decisions but has to consult the communities before taking action.

Declaration of parent lines with their passport data in breeder rights claims is essential to guaranteeing that farming communities that have contributed the varieties can be identified and given just compensation. Declaration of parent lines will also help other researchers using these varieties to develop new and/or improved varieties.

Farmers' rights include the right to breed new varieties and to sell seed. Farmers' seed sales account for over 70 per cent of the seed supply in India, helping to maintain both the price of the seed as well as the quality. Eliminating the farmer as a seed seller places him at the mercy of seed corporations as well as endangers the food security of the country.

IPR Reform in India

The real problem India is facing is that of the piracy of centuries of innovation and the discounting of our indigenous knowledge as *prior art* in consideration of inventiveness and novelty for patent applications. This denial of prior art and the phenomenon of biopiracy is of epidemic proportions and will continue in spite of our joining the PCT. As a result of our joining the PCT we can be in the insane situation of having to recognize Grace's patents on *neem*, RiceTec's patents on *basmati*, the Monsanto–USDA patent on the Terminator Technology since we have offered to recognize the rights of international patent applicants *before* getting our domestic laws in place and before enshrining the rights of the Indian tribal, peasant, indigenous health practitioner and consumer in our laws—especially the biodiversity law and the farmers' rights law.

The current trends in patenting have allowed patenting of seeds in addition to naturally occurring micro-organisms such as soil bacteria. Pharmaceutical corporations and western governments are patenting and claiming monopoly control over human genes, proteins and cell lines. For example, the US Department of Commerce patented the cell lines of a Panamanian Indian tribal woman who had resistance to cancer. This would have serious implications for the moral order. Multinational corporations have applied for patents on cows, which have been genetically engineered with human genes to produce 'human milk'. They have also applied for patents on sheep which have been genetically engineered to produce pharmaceuticals in their milk. Applications have even been made for mammary glands of women to be used as 'bioreactors' for the production of pharmaceuticals. Patents on animals including the human species is an assault on the moral order of a diverse society with diverse cultural and religious beliefs. This group of patent applications and exclusive marketing rights will lead to industrial farming of animals and increase the levels of cruelty already exhibited in factory farming.

Such concerns led the European Parliament to turn down on 1 March 1995, the patent directive that allowed patenting of life forms.

The present Patent (Amendment) Act in India allows patent applications for all substances to be used as pharmaceuticals and would therefore allow patenting of human genetic material. The new version of the Patents (Amendment) Act needs to explicitly state that such applications will not be considered. The new Patents (Amendment) Act needs to explicitly exclude patent applications for human genes, proteins and cell lines.

Multinational pharmaceutical companies have already taken out patents on ayurvedic drugs. If Exclusive Marketing Rights are granted in this area, Indian health care will be severely threatened since 70 per cent of the people in the country still depend on indigenous systems of medicine for maintaining their health status. Such patents will also deprive India of economic benefits that the country can derive through the Biodiversity Convention for being the source of material as well as knowledge. While patent applications and EMRs in this area need to be clearly excluded, a *sui generis* system of community intellectual rights protection needs to be evolved that recognizes the community innovation underlying these systems of medicine.

There have already been major movements in the country against patenting of seed and patenting of life forms. This democratic ground allows the government to introduce such grounds for exclusion in the consideration of applications of EMR now and patent applications later. Exclusive Marketing Rights should not be given for seeds and plant material, including genetically engineered seeds and plant material, and naturally occurring as well as genetically engineered microorganisms. All seeds and plant material should only be covered under a Plant Variety Protection Act which is based on farmers' rights as equal to breeders' rights in terms of innovation.

The Indian government's rush to enact modified laws in order to implement TRIPs is not justified. Many critical aspects of TRIPs are under review and the government should ensure that TRIPs is reviewed to guarantee protection of national and public interest and implement national laws only after it has played a leading role in reshaping the TRIPs Agreement. All the countries of Africa have demanded a five-year delay in implementation in TRIPs while these changes are effected. The date of 1 January 2000 as the deadline for implementation is itself under flux and India does not need to rush to implement TRIPs. As a member of WTO, India can join the African countries in changing the implementation period.

The collapse of the Seattle Round of WTO should be used by India to increase its national sovereign space in shaping national legislation and national economic policies.

The US, which is the country applying the maximum pressure to implement TRIPs and had initiated a TRIPs dispute against India, is itself going to vote on whether to remain a member of the WTO and whether to continue to pay dues to the Geneva-based organization. There is therefore no justification in exaggerating the role and power of WTO internationally and in our national affairs.

Given the ongoing review of TRIPs, the collapse of the Seattle Round of WTO and the worldwide challenge to US patent laws, the Government of India is not justified in rushing through with bad laws that are unnecessary, both in terms of their timing and content. The government is engaging in double standards, because while calling for exclusion for patents on life in the TRIPs review, it is hurriedly implementing legislation which allows patents on life and IPR monopolies in the vital sectors of food and medicine.

Patent laws have always been important in shaping the economy. In their expanded form covering all subject matter, including life forms, patent laws will spell life and death options for India's two-third majority who derive their livelihoods from biodiversity. The enclosure of our intellectual and biodiversity commons through patents is the ultimate colonization. This colonization is a threat to our survival.

Conclusion

Patents embody the political and economic arrangements of different periods of human history. In the colonial period, they were instruments of colonization and maintenance of colonial dependence. In the post-colonial period, patents became a reflection of our striving for economic freedom and political sovereignty.

As we enter a new millennium, we also enter a historical watershed. The patent regimes that are designed and shaped could reintroduce a new era of colonialism in which not only are we recolonized as a people, but all life forms are colonized.

Or we could challenge the patent paradigm that allows life forms to be treated as human inventions and corporate property, which allows piracy of centuries of innovation and indigenous creativity. Patents will be the prisms of our age, and how we shape our policy will shape the patent laws. If our political and economic systems descend into a free-fall for piracy and predation, patent laws will promote biopiracy and intellectual piracy, they will institutionalize bioserfdom and intellectual slavery. If we base our political and economic systems on democracy and diversity, patent laws will operate within the limits of rewarding genuine creativity and will not cross ethical and ecological limits that threaten the fabric of life in nature and society.

My intellectual and political energies have been dedicated to realizing the latter option of intellectual freedom for all people and ecological freedom for all beings. At the end of reading this book, I believe other individuals as well will realize the same.

Appendix
Patent Laws in India

A brief account of the major considerations which influenced patent laws in India, specially the 1970 Indian Patents Act.

When patents as exclusive rights were introduced in India, a major debate took place on whether the Company could grant such rights since this was the prerogative of the Crown in England.

In 1853, parliament granted this power to the Governor General-in-Council, with the prior consent of the Crown.

In 1856, Act VI was enacted '...for granting exclusive privileges to inventors', but it was repealed because it had not received the consent of the Court of Directors of the East India Company. Act XV of 1859 was the first Patent Act, more accurately called the law for 'exclusive privileges'. Through this Act, English patent holders could register their 'exclusive privileges' in India within twelve months of their claim in England.

In 1872, Act XIII was enacted on Patents and Designs Protection.

The Inventions and Design Act V of 1888 covered inventions displayed at exhibitions.

The Patent Debate in Independent India

The need to change colonial patent law was felt immediately after independence. The Bakshi Tek Chand Committee was established in (1948–50) by Resolution No. 233-IRP (6)/48) of the Ministry of Supply of the Government of India. The terms of the reference of the Committee were:

1. To survey and report on the working of the Patent System in India.

2. To examine the existing patent legislation for improving it, particularly with reference to the provisions concerned with the prevention of abuse of patent rights.
3. To consider whether any special restrictions should be imposed on patents regarding food and medicine.
4. To suggest steps for ensuring effective publicity to the patent system and to patent literature, particularly as regards patents obtained by Indian inventors.
5. To consider the necessity and feasibility of setting up a National Patents Trust.
6. To consider the desirability or otherwise of regulating the profession of patent agents.
7. To examine the working of the Patent Office and the services rendered by it to the public and make suitable recommendations for improvement; and
8. To report generally on any improvement that the Committee thinks fit to recommend for enabling the Indian Patent System to be more conducive to national interest by encouraging invention and the commercial development and use of inventions.

While the overall assumption was that the patent law and patent system need to be improved, on these issues the Committee's mandate was for review. This included the abuse of patent rights, the exclusion of food and medicine from patent systems, and the need for working and application of inventions for the national interest.

The Committee gave recommendations on what should not be patentable. The criteria of patentability included:

1. 'Invention' should be given a wider meaning...so as to include inventions capable of application for industrial uses, even if they are concerned with process only, and do not result in the manufacture of any article.
2. Substances prepared or produced by chemical processes or intended for food or medicine should not be patentable except when made by the invented processes or their obvious equivalents.
3. Inventions of which the primary or intended use would be contrary to law or morality should not be patentable.
4. To be 'useful' the invention should not only achieve the object claimed for it, but also be in the nature of technical advance on the existing stock of knowledge of the particular art in India.

In 1950, a Patents and Designs (Amendment) Bill was introduced in parliament. The object was to secure the national interests against any exercise or abuse which holders of patents coming from foreign countries may exercise to the detriment of India. Compulsory licensing was proposed for patents which created dependence on imports, prevented the development of indigenous industry and failed to meet domestic needs. The parliamentary debate of 1950 was the first democratic discussion on patents in India.

The next proposal of changes was made on 5 November 1952. In the parliamentary debate, V.P. Nayar stated, 'The law of patents has been bad, it has been on the imperialist pattern in which it was moulded right up to now'. According to him, patents killed development, they did not promote it.

The next stage of the patent debate was on 7 December 1953 in which it was proposed that the compulsory licensing provisions be extended to cover insecticides, fungicides and germicides. That insecticides were put in the same category as food and medicine was part of the Nehruvian model of following the industrialized countries in their path of development, including the poisonous path of pesticides. Justifying the extension of 'compulsory licensing' provisions for food and medicine to insecticides, the Minister of Commerce, Karmakar, stated, 'Considering the vital part that agriculture plays in our economy, it is most important that the manufacture of these insecticides etc. on a large scale should be encouraged and that we should not allow any loophole in our legislation which can be exploited by interested people. It is for this purpose that it is proposed to take powers to enable the Controller to issue these licenses for these articles exactly in the same manner as for food, medicine and surgical and curative devices.'

The debate on patents assumed that patents on food, medicine and pesticides should be granted, but the Government should use its powers to grant compulsory licenses. The value of compulsory licenses in the context of large monopolies was seriously questioned, as was the assumption that Indian research was independent of global corporate power. V.P. Nayar insisted that in spite of changes the law of patents in India was always working to the advantage of certain foreign nationals. The research on fungicides at the Central Rice Research Institute was being done by Imperial Chemical

Industries (ICI). Lever Brothers sales of Rs 2200 crore was five times India's budget. Allowing others to work the patent was meaningless for correcting the power of these giant corporations.

The Patents Bill of 1953 lapsed with the Lok Sabha dissolution. However, the 1911 Act did get amended with provisions for compulsory licensing. In April 1957, a Committee headed by N. Rajgopala Ayyangar was appointed and in 1959 it submitted a report on the 'Revision of the Patents Law'. The Ayyangar Committee stated that the monopoly created by the patent system was merely a system of market control which prevented India's development and prevented the public from having access to cheaper alternatives because of patent protection. The Ayyangar Committee recommended that the public interest could be safeguarded by the following provisions:

1. By defining with precision inventions which should be patentable and by rendering unpatentable certain inventions, the grants of patents to which will be detrimental to research or industrial progress or to national health or well-being.
2. By expanding the scope of anticipation so as to comprehend not merely what is known or published in this country but also what is known and published outside India.
3. By providing remedies for the evils which India, in common with other countries, experiences from foreign-owned patents which are not worked in the country, but which are held either to block industries of that country to secure a monopoly of importation.
4. By providing special provisions as regards the licensing of patents for inventions relating to food and medicine.
5. By providing remedies for other forms of abuse resorted to by patentees, to secure a more extended monopoly or a monopoly for a longer duration than what the statute grants.

Following the Ayyangar Committee recommendations, twelve years passed before Bill No. 62 was introduced in the Lok Sabha as Patents Bill 1965. The 1965 patent debate also focussed on monopolies in food and medicine. The Rajya Sabha discussed the proposal for a joint committee and agreed to it in December 1965. The report of the Committee was never debated because the Lok Sabha was dissolved and the 1965 Bill lapsed with it.

A new Bill was introduced in the new parliament in 1967. This Bill was also sent to a joint committee and brought to parliament in 1970.

The Indian Patent Act, 1970

The Patent Act of independent India was based on restricting the market exclusively built into the 1911 Act which blocked domestic production by allowing imports of patented products. The 1970 Act was committed to the following principles:

1. That patents are granted to encourage inventions and to secure that the inventions are worked in India on a commercial scale and to the fullest extent that is reasonably practicable without undue delay, and
2. That they are not granted merely to enable patentees to enjoy a monopoly for the importation of the patented article.

The major elements of the 1970 Act which served the public were:

1. Exclusion of food and medicine
2. Shorter life of patent
3. The discounting of import as working of a patent
4. Compulsory licensing.

Food and medicine could not be monopolized. This was achieved by not allowing patents for products themselves (product patents) but only for the process or method of manufacture (process patent). This exclusion is contained in Section 5 which states:
  In the case of inventions,

1. Claiming substances intended for use, or capable of being used, as food or medicine or drug; or
2. Relating to substances prepared or produced by chemical process (including alloys, optical glass, semiconductors and inter-metallic compounds) no patent shall be granted in respect of claims for the substances themselves, but claims for the method or process of manufacture shall be patentable.

This basically implies that no one could have monopolies over food and drugs, since others could produce the same product by a different process. This single clause allowed India to emerge as a pharmaceutical giant and allowed drug prices in India to become the lowest in the world.

The definition of food in the Indian Patent Act (Section 2(1)(g)) is:

> Meaning any article of nourishment and includes any substances intended for the use of babies, invalids or convalescents as an article of food or drink.

Section 2(1) defines 'medicine and drugs' as:

1. All medicines for internal or external use of human beings or animals.
2. All substances intended to be used in the diagnosis, treatment, mitigation or prevention of diseases in human beings or animals.
3. All substances intended to be used in the maintenance of public health, or the prevention or control of any epidemic disease among human beings or animals.
4. Insecticides, germicides, fungicides, weedicides and all other substances intended to be used for the protection and preservation of plants.
5. All chemical substances which are ordinarily used as intermediates in the preparation or manufacture of any of the medicines or substances referred to.

In addition to excluding patents for food and medicine, the 1970 Act also excludes certain areas from patentability by having clear principles for what will not be considered patentable. This includes (in Section 3 of the Patent Act):

1. An invention which is frivolous or which claims anything obviously contrary to well established natural laws.
2. An invention the primary or intended use of which would be contrary to law or morality or injurious to public health.
3. The mere discovery of a scientific principle or the formulation of an abstract theory.
4. The mere discovery of any new property or new use for a known substance or the mere use of a known process, machine or apparatus unless such known process results in a new reactant;

5. A substance obtained by a mere admixture resulting only in the aggregation of the properties.

6. The mere arrangements or rearrangements or duplication of known devices each functioning independently of another in a known way.

7. A method or processing of testing applicable during the process of manufacture for rendering the machine, apparatus or other equipment more efficient or for the improvement or restoration of the existing machine, apparatus or other equipment or for the improvement or control of manufacture.

8. A method of agriculture or horticulture.

9. Any process for the medicinal, surgical, curative, prophylactic or other treatment of human beings or any process for a similar treatment of animals or plants to render them free from disease or to increase their economic value or the value of their products.

Besides these broad areas of what did not count as an 'invention' and hence was not patentable subject area, the 1970 Act was also equipped with extensive rights and powers for government to prevent abuse of patents, and protect the public interest. The most important mechanisms for protection of the interest of the public were compulsory licensing, licenses of right, and revocation. The reason these rights were considered necessary was because in the Third World most patents are taken by foreigners who have no intention of making or manufacturing the product or using the process in the country. The object of getting a patent is merely as an import monopoly. This hurts producers by blocking production. It hurts consumers by raising prices of essential goods and preventing others from importing the product. To defend the rights of the public, the government can limit import monopolies by the provisions for compulsory licensing and licenses of right and revocation.

COMPULSORY LICENSING

Sections 84(1) and 84(5) of the Indian Patent Act state that after three years of the granting of a patent, any person may apply to the Controller of Patents for a compulsory license if the reasonable requirements of the public with respect to the patented invention have not been satisfied or that the patented invention is not available to the public at a reasonable price.

LICENSES OF RIGHTS

In cases where it is felt that 'the reasonable requirements of the public have not been satisfied or that the patented invention is not available to the public at a reasonable price' (Section 86 (1)), the government, through the Controller, can grant every one the right to use the patent right. In areas such as food, medicine, drugs, or chemical processes, there is provision of an automatic license of right 3 years after the granting of process patents.

In both 'license of right' and 'automatic license of right' cases any one any ask the patent holder for a license as a matter of right, and the Controller can intervene on terms and conditions of the license if the patent holder and applicant are not able to agree.

REVOCATION

If the government feels that the reasonable requirements of the public have not been met, over and above the granting of compulsory licenses and licenses of rights, the government may revoke the patent (Article 89). Patents can also be revoked if its exercise is mischievous to the state or generally prejudicial to the public (Article 60).

The guidelines for whom the reasonable requirements of the public are not being met are given in Article 90. The following are the circumstances under which the reasonable requirements of the public will be taken as not being met.

Firstly,

1. An existing trade or industry or its development, or any new trade or industry or the trade and industry of any person or classes of persons in India is prejudiced.
2. The demand for the patented article is not being met to an adequate extent or on reasonable terms from manufacture in India.
3. A market for the export of the patented article manufactured in India is not being supplied or developed.
4. The establishment or development of commercial activity in India is prejudiced (Section 90a).

Secondly, if a patent holder imposes extraneous conditions so that manufacture, sale or use of materials not projected by the patent is restrained and any trade or industry in India is prejudiced (Section 90b).

Thirdly, when a patented invention is not being adequately worked in India (Section 90c).

Fourthly, when the demand for the patented article in India is being met largely by imports by the patentee.

Fifthly, when the patentee prevents the working of the patent on a commercial scale because the article is being imported.

In spite of these clauses, the patent scene in India has continued to be dominated by foreigners. As Rajeev Dhawan states, 'The patent system was the playground of foreign firms. There was no indication that these firms were manufacturing in India. India was a dumping ground for goods, and patent power provided the leverage whereby multinationals could make lucrative collaborative deals.'

From 1856 when the first patent protection was given to patents in the sub-continent, few Indians had filed applications. In 1856, there were no Indians among the thirty-three applicants. In 1990, out of 492 applicants, forty-five were Indians. In 1910, sixty-two out of 667 were Indians. In 1949, 345 out of 1725 were Indians.

Since independence the pattern remains the same, with foreigners holding the majority of patent claims. The proportion of Indian patent holders did go up after the introduction of the 1970 Act, but the trend towards foreign domination has been reestablished. In 1986–87, of the total number of patents (12,063), 83.3 per cent were owned by foreigners.

In most cases, in spite of the possibility of compulsory licensing and licenses of right, patent monopolies have not been restricted. Very few applications have been made for compulsory licensing since 1970 and many patents have not being worked in India.

Therefore, even though the clauses in the 1970 Act exist to prevent monopolies, India's various attempts to stem the tide of foreign domination through the Patent Act of 1970 have not served as an effective barrier to such domination.

References

Bija: The Seed, Nos. 17 & 18, RFSTE, 1996.

Brian Belcher and **Geoffrey Hawtin**, *A Patent on Life: Ownership of Plant and Animal Research*, IDRC, 1991.

Leora Broydo, 'A Seedy Business', http:/www.mojones.com/news-wire.

W.M. Cohen and **R. Levin**, 'Empirical Studies of Innovative Activity', in P. Stoneman, ed., *Handbook of the Economics of Innovation and Technical Change*, Handbook of Industrial Organization.

John Croome, *Reshaping the World Trade System: A History of the Uruguay Round*, WTO, 1995.

Paul A. David, 'Intellectual Property Institutions and Panda's Thumb: Patents, Copyrights and Trade Secrets in Economic Theory and History', in NRC, *Global Dimensions of Intellectual Property Rights in Science and Technology*, National Academy Press, 1993.

Rajeev Dhawan, Lindsay Harris and **Gopal Jain**, 'Whose Interest? Independent India's Patent Law and Policy', in *Conquest by Patent: On Patent Law and Policy*, National Working Group on Patent Laws, New Delhi, 1988.

David Dickson, 'MIT Agrees to Accept Whitehead Grant: Faculty Votes Yes, but Strings Remain', *Nature*, 28 November 1981.

James Enyart, 'A GATT Intellectual Property Code', *Les Nouvelles*, June 1990.

P.J. Federico, 'Origin and Early History of Patents', *Journal of the Patent Office Society*, 1929, Vol. II, pp 293–95.

GAIA and **GRAIN**, 'Global Trade and Biodiversity in Conflict', No.3, October 1998.

S.C. Gilfillan, 'Invention and the Patent System', Joint Economic Committee, US Congress, 1964.

GRAIN, 'TRIPs versus Biodiversity: What to Do with the 1999 Review of Article 27.3(b)', 1999.

Fransesca Grifo, et. al., 'The Origins of Prescription Drugs', in Fransesca Grifo and Joshua Rosenthal, eds, *Biodiversity and Human Health*, Island Press, 1997.

The Hindu, 'Protect Private Sector in Farm Research: Glickman', 30 January 1996.

Djedal Kadir, *Columbus and the Ends of the Earth*, University of California, 1992.

B.K. Keayla, 'Conquest by Patents', *TRIPs Agreement on Patent Laws: Impact on Pharmaceuticals and Health for All*, Centre for Study of Global Trade System and Development, 1998.

Martin Kenney, *Biotechnology: The University-Industrial Complex*, Yale University Press.

Andrew Kimbrell, *The Human Body Shop: The Engineering and Marketing of Life*, HarperCollins Publishers, 1993.

Michael Kremer, 'A Mechanism for Encouraging Innovation', HIID Discussion Paper No. 533, May 1996.

Sheldon Krimsky, *Biotechnics and Society: The Rise of Industrial Genetics*, Praeger, 1991.

John Locke and **Peter Caslett**, eds, *Two Treatises of Government*, Cambridge University Press, 1967.

Edwin Mansfield, 'Intellectual Property, Technology and Economic Growth', in Francis W. Rushing and Carole Ganz Brown, eds, *Intellectual Property Rights in Science, Technology and Economic Performance*, Westview, 1990.

Barbara Mintzes, *Blurring the Boundaries: New Trends in Drug Promotion*, HAI, 1998.

NRC, *Global Dimensions of Intellectual Property Rights in Science and Technology*, National Academy Press, 1993.

Surendra Patel, 'Indian Patent Act, 1970', Paper presented at National Seminar on the Patent System in India organized by the National Working Group on Patent Laws, New Delhi, 22 November 1988.

RAFI, *Conserving Indigenous Knowledge: Integrating Two Systems of Innovation*, UNDP, 1994.

———, Occasional Paper, Vol. I, No.5, December 1994.

Resurgence, No. 195, July–August, Third World Network, 1999.

RFSTE, *Monsanto: Peddling 'Life Sciences' or 'Death Sciences'?*, 1998.

Pratiman Sarkar, 'Maharaja's New Clothes', *A Patent Chronicle*, Publication and Information Directorate, 1995.

Robert Sherwood, *Intellectual Property and Economic Development*, Westview Press.

Vandana Shiva, *Creating Seed Monopolies*, RFSTE, 1993.

———, *Protecting our Biological and Intellectual Heritage in the Age of Biopiracy*, RFSTNRP, 1996.

———, *Future of our Seeds, Future of our Farmers: Agricultural Biodiversity, Intellectual Property Rights and Farmers' Rights*, RFSTNRP, 1996.

———, *Biopiracy: The Plunder of Nature and Knowledge*, South End Press, 1997.

———, *Betting on Biodiversity: Why Genetic Engineering Will Not Feed the Hungry*, RFSTE, 1998.

Vandana Shiva and **Radha Holla-Bhar**, *Protection of Plants, People and Intellectual Rights: Proposed amendments to the Draft Plant Varieties Act, 1993*, RFSTE, 1993.

Vandana Shiva and **Afsar Jafri**, *Seeds of Suicide*, RFSTE, 1997.

Vandana Shiva, Afsar H. Jafri, Gitanjali Bedi and **Radha Holla-Bhar**, *The Enclosure and Recovery of the Commons: Biodiversity, Indigenous Knowledge and Intellectual Property Rights*, RFSTE, 1997.

Vandana Shiva, Vanaja Ramprasad, Pandurang Hegde, Omkar Krishnan and **Radha Holla-Bhar**, 'The Seed Keepers', *Navdanya*, 1995.

Timothy Swanson, ed., *Intellectual Property Rights and Biodiversity Conservation*, 1995.

UNDP, 'Questioning the Ownership of Knowledge', Human Development Project, 1999.

UNCTAD, 'Trends in International Transfer of Technology in Developing Countries', UNCTAD, 1986.

————, 'Transnational Corporations, Market Structure and Competition Policy: Overview', *World Investment Report, 1997*, UNCTAD, 1997.

Fred Warshofsky, *The Patent Wars*, John Wiley and Sons, 1994.

Claudia Von Werlhof, 'Women and Nature in Capitalism', in Mies Maria, ed., *Women: The Last Colony*, Zed Books, 1989.

Working Group on Patent Law, 'In Conquest', New Delhi, 1989.

N.B. Zaveer, 'Patents for Medicine: Balanced Patent Law—The Need of the Hour', Indian Drug Manufacturers' Association, 1998.

THE GLOBAL ISSUES SERIES

Already available

In preparation

Calestous Juma, *The New Genetic Divide: Biotechnology in the Age of Globalization*

John Madeley, *Food for All: The Need for a New Agriculture*

Jeremy Seabrook, *The Future of Culture: Can Human Diversity Survive in a Globalized World?*

David Sogge, *Give and Take: What's the Matter with Foreign Aid?*

Keith Suter, *Curbing Corporate Power: How Can We Control Transnational Corporations?*

Oscar Ugarteche, *A Level Playing Field: Changing the Rules of the Global Economy*

Nedd Willard, *The Drugs War: Is This the Solution?*

For full details of this list and Zed's other subject and general catalogues, please write to: The Marketing Department, Zed Books, 7 Cynthia Street, London N1 9JF, UK or email Sales@zedbooks. demon.co.uk

Visit our website at: www.zedbooks.demon.co.uk

Participating Organizations

Both ENDS A service and advocacy organization which collaborates with environment and indigenous organizations, both in the South and in the North, with the aim of helping to create and sustain a vigilant and effective environmental movement.

Damrak 28-30, 1012 LJ Amsterdam, The Netherlands
Phone: +31 20 623 0823   Fax: +31 20 620 8049
Email: info@bothends.org
Website: www.bothends.org

Catholic Institute for International Relations (CIIR) CIIR aims to contribute to the eradication of poverty through a programme that combines advocacy at national and international level with community-based development.

Unit 3, Canonbury Yard, 190a New North Road, London N1 7BJ, UK
Phone +44 (0)20 7354 0883   Fax +44 (0)20 7359 0017
Email: ciir@ciir.org
Website: www.ciir.org

Corner House The Corner House is a UK-based research and solidarity group working on social and environmental justice issues in North and South.

PO Box 3137, Station Road, Sturminster Newton, Dorset DT10 1YJ, UK
Tel.: +44 (0)1258 473795   Fax: +44 (0)1258 473748
Email: cornerhouse@gn.apc.org
Website: www.cornerhouse.icaap.org

Council on International and Public Affairs (CIPA) CIPA is a human rights research, education and advocacy group, with a particular focus on economic and social rights in the USA and elsewhere around the world. Emphasis in recent years has been given to resistance to corporate domination.

777 United Nations Plaza, Suite 3C, New York, NY 10017, USA
Tel. +1 212 972 9877   Fax +1 212 972 9878
E-mail: cipany@igc.org
Website: www.cipa-apex.org

Dag Hammarskjöld Foundation The Dag Hammarskjöld Foundation, established 1962, organises seminars and workshops on social, economic and cultural issues facing developing countries with a particular focus on alternative and innovative solutions. Results are published in its journal *Develpment Dialogue*.

Övre Slottsgatan 2, 753 10 Uppsala, Sweden.
Tel.: +46 18 102772   Fax: +46 18 122072
e-mail: secretariat@dhf.uu.se
Website: www.dhf.uu.se

Development GAP   The Development Group for Alternative Policies is a Non-Profit Development Resource Organization working with popular organizations in the South and their Northern partners in support of a development that is truly sustainable and that advances social justice.

927 15th Street NW, 4th Floor, Washington, DC, 20005, USA
Tel.: +1 202 898 1566   Fax: +1 202 898 1612
E-mail: dgap@igc.org
Website: www.developmentgap.org

Focus on the Global South   Focus is dedicated to regional and global policy analysis and advocacy work. It works to strengthen the capacity of organizations of the poor and marginalized people of the South and to better analyse and understand the impacts of the globalization process on their daily lives.

C/o CUSRI, Chulalongkorn University, Bangkok 10330, Thailand
Tel.: +66 2 218 7363 Fax: +66 2 255 9976
Email: Admin@focusweb.org
Website: www.focusweb.org

Inter Pares   Inter Pares, a Canadian social justice organization, has been active since 1975 in building relationships with Third World development groups and providing support for community-based development programs. Inter Pares is also involved in education and advocacy in Canada, promoting understanding about the causes, effects and solutions to poverty.

58 rue Arthur Street, Ottawa, Ontario, K1R 7B9 Canada
Phone +1 613 563 4801   Fax +1 613 594 4704

Public Interest Research Centre   PIRC is a research and campaigning group based in Delhi which seeks to serve the information needs of activists and organizations working on macro-economic issues concerning finance, trade and development.

142 Maitri Apartments, Plot No. 28, Patparganj, Delhi 110092, India
Phone: +91 11 2221081/2432054   Fax: +91 11 2224233
Email: kaval@nde.vsnl.net.in

Third World Network TWN is an international network of groups and individuals involved in efforts to bring about a greater articulation of the needs and rights of peoples in the Third World; a fair distribution of the world's resources; and forms of development which are ecologically sustainable and fulfil human needs. Its international secretariat is based in Penang, Malaysia.

228 Macalister Road, 10400 Penang, Malaysia
Tel.: +60 4 226 6159   Fax: +60 4 226 4505
Email: twnet@po.jaring.my
Website: www.twnside.org.sg

Third World Network–Africa TWN–Africa is engaged in research and advocacy on economic, environmental and gender issues. In relation to its current particular interest in globalization and Africa, its work focuses on trade and investment, the extractive sectors and gender and economic reform.

2 Ollenu Street, East Legon, PO Box AN19452, Accra-North, Ghana.
Tel.: +233 21 511189/503669/500419   Fax: +233 21 511188
email: twnafrica@ghana.com

World Development Movement (WDM) The World Development Movement campaigns to tackle the causes of poverty and injustice. It is a democratic membership movement that works with partners in the South to cancel unpayable debt and break the ties of IMF conditionality, for fairer trade and investment rules, and for strong international rules on multinationals.

25 Beehive Place, London SW9 7QR, UK
Tel.: +44 (0)20 7737 6215   Fax: +44 (0)20 7274 8232
E-mail: wdm@wdm.org.uk
Website: www.wdm.org.uk

THIS BOOK IS ALSO AVAILABLE
IN THE FOLLOWING COUNTRIES

EGYPT

MERIC
(The Middle East Readers'
Information Center)
2 Bahgat Ali Street,
Tower D/Apt. 24
Zamalek
Cairo
Tel: 20 2 735 3818/736 3824
Fax: 20 2 736 9355

FIJI

University Book Centre,
University of South Pacific,
Suva
Tel: 679 313900
Fax: 679 303265

GHANA

EPP Book Services,
PO Box TF 490,
Trade Fair,
Accra
Tel: 233 21 773087
Fax: 233 21 779099

MOZAMBIQUE

Sul Sensações
PO Box 2242,
Maputo
Tel: 258 1 421974
Fax: 258 1 423414

NAMIBIA

Book Den
PO Box 3469
Shop 4, Frans Indongo Gardens
Windhoek
Tel: 264 61 239976
Fax: 264 61 234248

NEPAL

Everest Media Services,
GPO Box 5443, Dillibazar
Putalisadak Chowk

Kathmandu
Tel: 977 1 416026
Fax: 977 1 250176

PAPUA NEW GUINEA

Unisearch PNG Pty Ltd
Box 320, University
National Capital District
Tel: 675 326 0130
Fax: 675 326 0127

RWANDA

Librairie Ikirezi
PO Box 443
Kigali
Tel/Fax: 250 71314

SUDAN

The Nile Bookshop
New Extension Street 41
P O Box 8036
Khartoum
Tel: 249 11 463749

TANZANIA

TEMA Publishing Co Ltd
PO Box 63115
Dar Es Salaam
Tel: 255 22 2113608
Fax: 255 22 2110472

UGANDA

Aristoc Booklex Ltd
PO Box 5130, Kampala Road
Diamond Trust Building
Kampala
Tel: 256 41 344381/349052
Fax: 256 41 254867

ZAMBIA

UNZA Press
PO Box 32379
Lusaka
Tel: 260 1 290409
Fax: 260 1 253952